Africa and the Decolonisation of State-Religion Policies

Comparative Discrimination Law

Volumes published in this Brill Research Perspectives title are listed at *brill.com/rpcd*

Africa and the Decolonisation of State-Religion Policies

By

J. Osogo Ambani

BRILL

LEIDEN | BOSTON

This paperback book edition is simultaneously published as issue 4.2 (2020) of *Comparative Discrimination Law*, DOI:10.1163/24522031-12340009.

Typeface for the Latin, Greek, and Cyrillic scripts: "Brill". See and download: brill.com/brill-typeface.

ISBN 978-90-04-44641-0 (paperback)
ISBN 978-90-04-44642-7 (e-book)

This book is printed on acid-free paper and produced in a sustainable manner.

Contents

Africa and the Decolonisation of State-Religion Policies

John Osogo Ambani
Strathmore University
ambaniosogo@yahoo.com
jambani@strathmore.edu

Abstract

This volume in the Brill Research Perspectives in Comparative Discrimination Law addresses religion, the State and discrimination. The long history of state-religion interaction has yielded four main interface models: the religious state; the state with an established religion; the antireligious state; and the secular state. African states have drawn from these four models when struggling to manage state-religion relations. This volume argues that the African countries studied here, Kenya, Nigeria and Uganda, apply the concept of state-secularism without having their triple heritage, which encompasses African religion, Islam and Christianity, in contemplation. This volume proposes that the best way to realise the full flowering of the triple heritage is to erect the three pillars of Charles Taylor's definition of state-secularism, which in this case should entail i) the freedom to have and to manifest religious beliefs, ii) equal treatment of religion, and iii) and efforts toward an all-inclusive state identity.

Keywords

comparative law – discrimination – religion – state – African religion – Ali Mazrui – Islam – Christianity – Charles Taylor – secularism – equal treatment of religion – triple heritage

Introduction

This volume is the ninth in the Brill Research Perspectives series concerning comparative discrimination law. This series addresses comparative discrimination issues both horizontally (overarching frameworks) and vertically (specific

 | DOI:10.1163/9789004446427_002

issues within discrimination law). Topics include unlawful discrimination on the basis of race, sex, religion, age, disability, gender, sexual orientation, as well as intersectionality – at national, regional, and international levels. Theoretical as well as more pragmatic approaches, such as the use of active measures to combat structural discrimination and proving discrimination claims with empirical evidence, are also explored. Law by its nature is bound by culture and language, and the effort in the series has been made to examine issues of discrimination from different jurisdictions.

This volume in the Brill Research Perspectives in Comparative Discrimination Law addresses religion and the State from the lens of comparative antidiscrimination law. The long history of state-religion interaction has yielded four main interface models: the religious state; the state with an established religion; the antireligious state; and the secular state. African states have drawn from these four models when struggling to manage state-religion relations. This volume argues that the African countries studied here, Kenya, Nigeria and Uganda, apply the concept of state-secularism without having their triple heritage, which encompasses African religion, Islam and Christianity, in contemplation. This volume proposes that the best way to realise the full flowering of the triple heritage is to erect the three pillars of Charles Taylor's definition of state-secularism, which in this case should entail i) the freedom to have and to manifest religious beliefs, ii) equal treatment of religion, and iii) and efforts toward an all-inclusive state identity.

The editors welcome suggestions as to authors and jurisdictions outside those presented in the volumes to date. This series is to run for ten years of quarterly volumes, with the ambition to achieve a broad approach to comparative discrimination law issues.

Part 1: State-Religion Relations[1]

The long history of state-religion interaction has yielded four main interface models: the religious state; the state with an established religion; the antireligious state; and the secular state. African states have drawn from these four models when struggling to manage state-religion relations. This volume argues that the African countries studied here, Kenya, Nigeria and Uganda, apply the concept of state-secularism without having their triple heritage, which

1 The author wishes to warmly thank Arnold Nciko (Strathmore University student) and Sydney Tambasi (Kenyatta University student) for their assistance when researching this volume.

encompasses African religion, Islam and Christianity, in contemplation. This volume proposes that the best way to realise the full flowering of the triple heritage is to erect the three pillars of Charles Taylor's definition of state-secularism, which in this case should entail i) the freedom to have and to manifest religious beliefs, ii) equal treatment of religion, and iii) and efforts toward an all-inclusive state identity, in essence decolonising state-religion policies.

Under the first model of state-religion relations, a religious state usually founds its laws, policies and programmes on the theological doctrine of the preferred denomination.[2] Saudi Arabia and the Vatican typify this model.[3] In Saudi Arabia, the 'regime derives its power from the Holy Qur'an and the Prophet's Sunnah' which rule over the Constitution and all other State laws.[4] Most Arabic countries in Africa have attempted versions of Saudi Arabia's approach. Sub-Sahara Africa's Zambia is a rare example of a Christian religious state in the region.[5] The second model, a state with an established religion, although it officially favours one religious denomination, runs its affairs ordinarily on secular principles.[6] Examples in this regard include Denmark, England and Greece.[7] None of Africa's 54 states operates on this model. The third typology, an antireligious state, like China, Cuba and North Korea, is officially averse to the idea of religion and therefore founds its governance philosophy from secular or neutral springs.[8] Again, Africa has not followed this model.

Many Sub-Saharan African states including Kenya, Nigeria and Uganda are usually classified under the fourth model, as secular states.[9] Donald Smith defines a secular state as one

> [w]hich guarantees individual and corporate freedom of religion, deals with the individual as a citizen irrespective of his religion, is not

2 Kuru, AT. Kuru, AT. "Passive and Assertive Secularism: Historical Conditions, Ideological Struggles, and State Policies towards Religion." *World Politics*, vol. 59, no. 4, p. 570.

3 Kuru, AT. *Secularism and State Policies toward Religion: The United States, France, and Turkey*. Cambridge University Press, 2009, pp. 247–253.

4 Article 7 of Saudi Arabia's Constitution of 1992 with Amendments through 2005. Generated from the repository of the comparative constitutions project, constituteproject.org. Accessed on 30 March 2015.

5 Preamble, *Constitution of Zambia*, (1996).

6 Kuru, AT. *Secularism and State Policies toward Religion: The United States, France, and Turkey*. p. 570.

7 Kuru, AT. *Secularism and State Policies toward Religion*. pp. 247–253.

8 Kuru, AT. *Secularism and State Policies toward Religion*. p. 570.

9 Ranger, Terrence O. "Religious Movements and Politics in Sub-Saharan Africa." *African Studies Review*, vol. 29, no. 2, 1986, pp. 1–69.

> constitutionally connected to a particular religion nor does it seek either to promote or interfere with religion.[10]

Similarly, Fineface Ogoloma observes that:

> [t]he secular state views the individual as a citizen and not as a member of a particular religious group. Religion becomes entirely irrelevant in defining the terms of citizenship; its rights and duties are not affected by the individual religious beliefs.[11]

Osita Ogbu visualises the modern idea of secularism as an attempt towards the separation of religion from politics, 'so that the state's existence is not justified by theology'.[12] Is-haq Oloyede regards a secular state as one that develops its moral values independent of religion.[13] In these senses, state-secularism carries the meaning of divorcing religion from law, government and politics.[14]

Although the interplay between state and religion tends to be so fluid in liberal constitutions that the 'secular state' evades a concise definition, there seems to be consonance in literature that state-secularism is a system whereby a) religion is subjected to the jurisdiction of the state, b) state-identity is representative of the religious diversity of the people, c) there is a separation between religion and state, law and politics, and d) individuals and groups enjoy the right to freedom of conscience, religion and worship.[15] Thus, France, Turkey and the US are secular states because '(1) their legal and judicial processes are out of institutional religious control, and (2) they establish neither

---

10 Eugene, Smith. D. "India as a Secular State." 1963, p. 4, as cited in Chiriyankandath, J. "Creating a Secular State in a Religious Country: The debate in the Indian Constituent Assembly." *Commonwealth and Comparative Politics*, vol. 38, no. 2, 2000, pp. 1–24.

11 Ogoloma, F. "Secularism in Nigeria: An assessment." *International Journal of Arts and Humanities*, vol. 1, no. 3, 2012, pp. 63–74.

12 Ogbu, ON. "Is Nigeria a secular state? Law, Human Rights and Religion in Context." *Transnational Human Rights Review*, vol. 1, 2014, p. 140.

13 Oloyede, I, Egbewole W. & Oloyede, H. "The operational complexities of "free exercise" and "adoption of religion" clauses in the Nigerian Constitution." presented at the 2015 Religious Freedom and Religious Pluralism in Africa: Prospects and Limitations Conference. p. 192.

14 See, also, A Davison, A. "Turkey, a "Secular" State? The Challenge of Description." *South Atlantic Quarterly*, vol. 102, no. 2/3, 2003, p. 342.

15 This description is subject to some exceptions as no state can claim to have liberated itself from religion completely. Therefore, it is safer to add a rider that no matter the extent of secularity, states continue to interact with religion in different ways.

an official religion nor atheism'.[16] The African study countries, Kenya, Nigeria and Uganda are also described as secular states.[17]

African states have drawn from these four models to manage state-religion relations. And when they fail to strike the right balance conflicts arise. Sometimes. It has not helped matters that many African countries have 'pronounced religious fragmentation and/or multiple cleavages'.[18] In Kenya, while African religion[19] has clamoured for recognition and inclusion since the colonial epoch,[20] constant rivalry and suspicion between Christians and Muslims have punctuated constitutional development.[21] The quite westernised aspirations of the Mainland, with a significant population of Christian converts, and the worries of the Islamic Sultanate of Zanzibar along the coast, preoccupied Kenya's independence deliberations in the early 1960s.[22] The resultant constitutional compromise remained as brittle in 2010 – when Kenya negotiated a new constitutional order – as it was in 1963 at independence.[23] That state-religion relations remain delicate is evidenced by the many disputes arbitrated in the Judiciary touching on important questions such as whether it

16 Kuru, AT. *Secularism and State Policies toward Religion*. p. 569.

17 Yesufu, Momoh Lawani. "The impact of religion on a secular state: the Nigerian experience." *Studia Historiae Ecclesiasticae*, 2016; Mazrui, Alamin. "Ethnicity and pluralism: the politicization of religion in Kenya." *Journal Institute of Muslim Minority Affairs*, vol. 14, no. 1 & 2, 1994, pp. 194; "The intention to adopt Islamic financing in emerging economies: evidence from Uganda." *Journal of Islamic Accounting and Business Research*, vol. 11, no. 3, p. 610.

18 Haynes, Jeffrey. "Religion, Ethnicity and Civil War in Africa: The Cases of Uganda and Sudan." *The Round Table*, vol. 98, no. 390, 2007, p. 307.

19 I use the singular form 'African religion' although I am aware of the debate concerning whether Africa has one religion or many religions. The titles of two main books on the subject are illustrative of the controversy. See, Mbiti, John Samuel. *African religions and philosophy*. East African Educational Publishers Ltd, 1969, pp. 15 and Magesa, Laurent. *African religion: The Moral Traditions of Abundant Life*. Paulines Publications Africa: Nairobi, 1998.

20 Muthiri, Githige. "The religious factor in Mau Mau with particular reference to Mau Mau Oaths", thesis submitted in part fulfilment for the Degree of Master of Arts in the University of Nairobi, February 1978.

21 Deacon, Gregory, et al. "Preaching politics: Islam and Christianity on the Kenya coast." *Journal of Contemporary African Studies*, vol. 35, no. 2, p. 151.

22 Brenna, James R. "Lowering the Sultan's Flag: Sovereignty and Decolonization in Coastal Kenya." *Comparative Studies in Society and History*, vol. 50, no. 4, 2008, pp. 831–861.

23 Tayob, Abubakar. "Kadhis Courts in Kenya's Constitutional Review (1998–2010): A Changing Approach to Politics and State Among Kenyan Muslim Leaders." *Islamic Africa*, vol. 4, no. 1, 2013, p. 103.

is constitutional for the State to fund Islamic courts,[24] whether religious freedom extends to donning religious attire in schools,[25] and whether schools can administer examinations or run ordinary programmes during recognised days of worship.[26]

If neglect for African religion and rivalry and suspicion between Christians and Muslims have defined Kenya's independence history, in Nigeria, such conflicts incline toward extremities. Jacob Omede and Andrew Abdul Omede list many instances of religious crises that span through the period of Nigeria's independence to recent history. These include, the

> [M]aitatsine riot in Kano in 1980, Maitatsine riot in Maiduguri in 1982, the same in Gombe in 1982 and Jimeta-Yola in 1984. Others were the inter-religious violence of 1987 in Kafanchan, Bauchi riot of 1991, Reinhard Bonnke riot in Kano in 1991, opposition of institution of sharia courts by some state governors that resulted to protest during Obasanjo's regime between 1999 and 2004, and the frequent burning of churches and killings that go on since the activities of "Boko Haram" in 2002.[27]

---

24 Funderburk, Bailey. "Between the Lines of Hegemony and Subordination: The Mombasa Kadhi's Court in Contemporary Kenya." *SIT Study Abroad*, 2010, p. 35.

25 *Republic v The Head Teacher, Kenya High School & Another Ex-parte SMY* (2012) eKLR; *Mohamed Fugicha v Methodist Church in Kenya & 3 others* (2016) eKLR; Wangai, Mukami. "Religious Pluralism in Practice: Defining Secularism in Kenya's Headscarf Cases." *Strathmore Law Journal*, vol. 3, 2017, pp. 177–186.

26 *Seventh Day Adventist Church (East Africa) Limited v Minister for Education & 3 others* [2014] eKLR.

27 Omede, Jacob and Omede, Andrew Abdul. "Terrorism and insecurity in Nigeria: Moral, values and religious education as panacea." *Journal of Education and Peace*, vol. 6, no. 11, 2015, p. 124. There is a history to these conflicts that goes as follows:

Nigeria, before it was colonized by the British, had a multi-cultural/multiethnic, multi-religious, multi-lingual and even multi political culture. As such, Nigeria was extremely heterogeneous and complex. In spite of these diversities in language, tribe and culture, "Nigeria" was forcibly put together by the West African constabulary force in 1900 without any consultation with the tribes concerned. The name Nigeria was coined by the Journalist wife of the first British Colonial ruler of Nigeria. Lord Frederick Lugard, who in 1914, completed the amalgamation of the Southern and Northern protectorates to form the country known and addressed as Nigeria. Since this geographical expression known as Nigeria was forcibly put together by a foreign power, its disparate units have not ceased to live in discomfort with one another. In fact, they live in mutual suspicion and distrust.

Uka, EM, Ethnic, Religious and Communal Conflict in Nigeria: Implications for Security, *Bassey Andah Journal*, vol. 1, 2008, p. 2. See also Achebe, Chinua. *Africa's Tarnished Name*, Penguin Classics, 2009, pp. 1–2.

Indeed, the Islamic State in West Africa (Boko Haram) – a pro-violence Islamic movement opposed to westernised education – has heightened Nigeria's ethno-religious conflict situation. There is also constant tension between the Northern states (a predominant Muslim constituency) and Southern states (with Christian majorities) and the establishment of Islamic law (Sharia) in Northern states and in others with large Muslim populations has elicited both heated intellectual contestations and genuine human rights concerns.

Uganda has similarly witnessed significant challenges in its state-religion relations. Uganda's most ferocious civil uprisings have pitied ethno-religious groups against each other. Inspired by African religion, Alice Lakwena guided the Holy Spirit Movement revolt against the Government of President Yoweri Museveni for over a year.[28] And just when these virulent battles were subsiding, Lakwena's cousin, Joseph Kony, took the baton to lead perhaps Uganda's most costly and convoluted civil war.[29] Relatedly,

> [t]he formation of the Uganda Islamic Revolutionary Party in 1993 to seek political power following the rise of Islamic fundamentalism was to be followed by the formation of the Allied Democratic Forces, an Islamic led and dominated rebel group that sought to use force to establish an Islamic state in Uganda.[30]

Partisan religious instruction has caused violence in certain learning institutions[31] and the question of Islamic civil courts in Uganda remains a potentially explosive issue.[32]

In this contribution, I argue that the African study countries apply the concept of state-secularism without having their triple heritage, which encompasses African religion, Islam and Christianity, in contemplation. This view is

28 Haynes, Jeffrey. "Religion, Ethnicity and Civil War in Africa: The Cases of Uganda and Sudan." *The Round Table*, vol. 98, no. 390, 2007, p. 312.

29 Haynes, Jeffrey. "Religion, Ethnicity and Civil War in Africa: The Cases of Uganda and Sudan." *The Round Table*, vol. 98, no. 390, 2007, p. 312.

30 Mwesigwa, Fred Sheldon "Religious Pluralism and Conflict as Issues in Religious Education in Uganda", LLM Thesis, The University of Leeds, School of Theology and Religious Studies, Leeds, November 2003.

31 Amone, Charles. "Contested Citizenship, Religious Discrimination and the Growth of Nubian Identity In Northern Uganda." *A Journal of Language, Culture and Communication* vol. 6, 2018, pp. 66–79.

32 Mujuzi, Jamil Ddamurila. "The Entrenchment of Qadis' Courts in the Ugandan Constitution." *International Journal of Law, Policy and the Family* vol. 26, no. 3, 2012, pp. 306–326.

undergirded by the premise that most applications of state-secularism in the African study countries favour the Christian faith, which during its tumultuous experiences in Europe survived the enlightenment, the reformation and like experiences socialised to co-exist with what are now called secular states. Additionally, due to the long history of Christendoms in Europe, Christian principles penetrated the colonial legal systems bequeathed to Africa at independence. The sustenance of the colonial legacy means that the Abrahamic faith has an upper hand in the state-religion relations' contest. The unhealthy collaboration between Christian missionaries and British colonial authorities also evidently consolidated the Christian advantage. Partially because of this, state-religion relations in the African study countries are sites both for ethno-religious conflict and struggle for religious equality. The obvious underdog in this uneven contest is African religion which has suffered major onslaughts since the colonial days.

I conclude in this volume that the state-religion policies of the African study countries must be true to the region's historical and current realities in which the triple heritage plays a prominent role. In this regard, I propose Charles Taylor's flexible approach to state-secularism, which classifies the concept of secularism in the three categories of the French revolutionary trinity: liberty, equality, fraternity.[33] The liberal component is visible in the requirement that 'no one must be forced in the domain of religion or basic belief'.[34] This is tantamount to what in the US constitutional set up is described as the 'free exercise' of religion.[35] The concept of secularism also entails 'equality between people of different faiths or basic belief' such that 'no religious outlook or (religious or areligious) Weltanschauung can enjoy a privileged status, let alone be adopted as the official view of the state'.[36] Finally, the 'fraternal' call of secularism enjoins all spiritual families together in the formulation of a common identity of state.[37] Seen in this light, the concept of state-secularism has more to do with the correct response of the democratic state to diversity than merely the relation of the state and religion.[38] It is also about equality and freedom.

To make these points, I first below explain the triple heritage theory. I then discuss the typical secular state models, France, Turkey and the US in relation

33 Taylor, C. "Why We Need a Radical Redefinition of Secularism" in Butler, J, Habermas, J, Taylor, C & West, C. "*The power of religion in the public sphere.*" 2011, p. 34.
34 Taylor, "Why We Need a Radical Redefinition of Secularism," p. 35.
35 Taylor, "Why We Need a Radical Redefinition of Secularism" p. 35. In the terms of the First Amendment to the US Constitution.
36 Taylor, "Why We Need a Radical Redefinition of Secularism," p. 35.
37 Taylor, "Why We Need a Radical Redefinition of Secularism" p. 35.
38 Taylor, "Why We Need a Radical Redefinition of Secularism," p. 36.

to the African study countries, Kenya, Nigeria and Uganda along defined parameters. The point here is to show that there is no particular, consistent or mandatory secular state practice. This sets the stage for criticising the African study countries for electing approaches of state-secularism that are detrimental to African religion and (sometimes) Islam. That discussion uses the right to freedom of religion in international law as the normative framework and the case study of educational institutions. Finally, I make the case for an all-inclusive understanding of the concept of state-secularism for the sake of the full-flowering of the triple heritage and more.

Part 2: A Theoretical Framework for the African Triple Heritage

I enter the debate on state-religion relations in Africa through the lenses of Ali Mazrui's triple heritage theory, which conceives that today's Africa is an amalgam of three major civilisations; indigenous Africanity, Islam and westernisation.[39] Indeed, prior to the coming of foreigners, Africans observed largely indigenous religious and cultural traditions. These nearly 'pure' societies were altered by the early visitors, imperialists and missionaries fundamentally.

The visitors interacted with indigenous institutions in many ways in the process distorting the continental socio-cultural landscape irrevocably. At the East African coast, the Portuguese and the Arabs introduced unique civilisations, and their legacy included inputting into the local languages, cultures, political and social systems, agriculture, architecture, trade, and religion.[40] Writing in this context, Anthony Oliver and Anthony Atmore chronicled that the discovery of early mosques built of ancient architectural material at the East African coast signify the presence of Arab traders in the region as early as the 9th century.[41] Adewale Taiwo recounted a similar experience in West Africa. According to this narrative, Islam had been firmly rooted in societies such as the Hausa by the 15th century. It is recorded that Islam walked to West

39 For a fuller treatment of the theory, see Mazrui, Ali A. *The Africans: A Triple Heritage*. Little, Brown and Company, Boston and Toronto, 1986.

40 See for instance, Martin BG. "Arab Migrations to East Africa in Medieval Times." *International Journal of African Historical Studies*, vol. 7, no. 3, 1974, pp. 367–367.

41 Atmore, Oliver. R.A. *Africa since 1800*. 5th ed., Cambridge University Press, 2005, pp. 30–31. It is also documented that 'between around 700 and 1500 AD, a majority of Muslim visitors to East Africa probably concerned with some aspect of trade.' See, for instance, Martin BG. "Arab Migrations to East Africa in Medieval Times." p. 375.

Africa alongside 40 Wangarawa traders, 'and during the reign of Muhammad Rumfa between 1463 and 1499, Islam was firmly rooted in Kano'.[42]

On their part, the imperialists occasioned phenomenal transformation through systematic imposition of foreign social, political and legal systems in which distinct western values were embedded. According to Lord Fredrick Lugard, the architect of British colonialism in east, west and parts of southern Africa,[43] the arrival of Europeans brought with it the mind and methods of Europe.[44] And the revolution was a fusion of material development, education and progress.[45] In imperial British Africa, for example, these outcomes were expected given that part of the 'dual mandate' British imperialism pursued was the 'civilisation of natives':

> [i]t was the task of civilisation to put an end to slavery, to establish courts of law, to inculcate in the natives a sense of individual responsibility, of liberty, of justice, and to teach their rulers how to apply these principles; above all, to see to it that the system of education should be such as to produce happiness and progress.[46]

Accompanying the British imperialists were the Christian missionaries who saw their religion and civilisation as superior, and thus bestowing upon them high responsibility to 'save' the native populations. Oginga Odinga, a freedom fighter and Kenya's first independence Vice President, thus narrated a close encounter with the 'saviours':

---

42 Taiwo, Edwale. E.A. "Justifications, Challenges And Constitutionality of The Penal Aspects of Shari'ah Law In Nigeria." *Griffith Law Review*, vol. 17, no. 1, 2008, pp. 183–202, 185. Regarding the introduction of Islamic customary law and its institutions, Yadudu has written: 'The Islamic legal order was brought to the pre-colonial part of Nigeria with the conversion of the people to Islam. This began in the 9th century with the Kanem Borno and spread in the 11th century to the rest of the region. However, the widespread application of the Islamic law and the formalisation of its judicial structures occurred only during the early part of the 19th century with the establishment of the Sokoto caliphate. This had occurred much earlier on a smaller scale under the Saifawa dynasty of Borno.' See Yadudu, Auwalu. H. "Colonialism and the Transformation of Islamic Law." *Journal of Legal Pluralism and Unofficial Law*, vol. 24, no. 2, 1992, p. 110.

43 Regarding the conquest of the relevant regions of Africa, Lugard has written: 'During the first half of these thirty years, it was my privilege to assist in some degree in bringing under British control portions of Nyasaland, East Africa, Uganda, and Nigeria ...' See Lugard, Frederick. J.D. *The Dual Mandate in British Tropical Africa*. 5th ed., 1965, p. 7.

44 Lugard, Frederick. J.D. *The Dual Mandate in British Tropical Africa*, p. 5.

45 Lugard, Frederick. J.D. *The Dual Mandate in British Tropical Africa*, p. 5.

46 Lugard, Frederick. J.D. *The Dual Mandate in British Tropical Africa*, p. 5.

> But over the years it dawned on me that I had listened to many preachers and they seemed, all of them, to preach one thing in common – the suppression of African customs. They were not satisfied to concentrate on the word of the Bible; they tried to use the word of God to judge African traditions. An African who followed his peoples' customs was condemned as heathen and anti-Christian. Those who lived among and mixed easily with the non-Christians who were, after all, the majority, were themselves dubbed heathen. Tribesmen who kept many animals were condemned as anti-Christian because the possession of many animals meant it was possible for a man to marry and pay dowry for several wives. Any man married to more than one woman was anti-Christian. Villagers who lived in the traditional fenced-in clusters of huts were anti-Christian; if they were followers of the church they would group their houses near the church building, it was thought.[47]

These developments are relevant to the African study countries all of which the British put under their control during the critical period.

Granted this background, Ali Mazrui rightly perceived contemporary Africa as the manifestation of the civilisational 'trinity'. He recounted that

> [t]he twentieth century witnessed the full flowering of Africa's *triple heritage* (Africanity, Islam, and westernization). This has developed into a major new paradigm for interpreting Africa – for viewing the continent as a convergence of three civilizations.[48]

The triple heritage theory visualizes Africa as a cultural bazaar where

---

47 Odinga, Odinga. *Not yet Uhuru: The Autobiography of Oginga*, East African Publishers, 1976, p. 42.

48 Mazrui, Ali. A. "The Re-Invention of Africa: Edward Said, VY Mudimbe, and Beyond." *Research in African Literatures*, vol. 36, no. 3, 2005, p. 36. Of this aspect, it has also been noted: 'Professor Ali Mazrui … argues that African culture today must be "understood best in terms of its 'triple heritage', of indigenous, Islam, and western forces, which had arisen out of an ancient confluence of indigenous, Semitic, and Greco-Roman forces." Consequently, the combination of these diverse cultures and current trends in globalization have immensely disturbed the purity of African customary values. Thus, an African cultural tradition may, therefore, mean much more than extant traditional practices. Indeed, it may impute a blend of traditional African values, western way of life, and even Asiatic values or traditional practices.' See Juma, L, "Reconciling African Customary Law and Human Rights in Kenya: Making a Case for Institutional Reformation and Revitalization of Customary Adjudication Processes." *Saint Thomas Law Review*, vol. 14, 2002, p. 475.

> [a] wide variety of ideas and values, drawn from different civilisations, compete for attention of potential African buyers. This marketing of cultures in Africa has been going on for centuries but a particularly important impact has come from the 'Semites' (especially Arabs and Jews) and the 'Caucasians' (especially western Europeans).[49]

Since colonialism, the cultural 'bazaar' that is Africa also doubles as a battlefield where indigenous African values and the forces of western civilisation have been set in opposition.[50] The western import is particularly significant in Africa since 'what Africa knows about itself, what different parts of Africa know about each other, have been profoundly influenced by the West'.[51] This western cultural vantage-point was catapulted by the colonial epoch which completed the full flowering of Africa's triple heritage with the 'Caucasian' civilisation as the more successful bidder in the cultural market and victor in the civilisational war.[52]

The result of this largely unidirectional pollination 'has been a remarkable pace of cultural dis-Africanisation and westernisation'.[53] Western values have infused not only the legal and political spheres but also the social and cultural aspects of Africa. With respect to state-religion relations, the African study countries emulate the western/northern heritage, for example, by formulating their state-religion relations along the lines of the US Constitution. The First Amendment of the US Constitution provides that '[C]ongress shall make no law respecting an establishment of religion, or prohibiting the free exercise thereof; ...' In similar vein, Kenya's 2010 Constitution provides that '[t]here shall be no State religion'.[54] Equally, the 1999 Constitution of Nigeria states that

49 Mazrui, Ali. A. "The Re-Invention of Africa: Edward Said, VY Mudimbe, and Beyond." pp. 76 and 97. Of this aspect, it has also been noted: 'Professor Ali Mazrui ... argues that African culture today must be "understood best in terms of its 'triple heritage', of indigenous, Islam, and western forces, which had arisen out of an ancient confluence of indigenous, Semitic, and Greco-Roman forces." Consequently, the combination of these diverse cultures and current trends in globalisation has immensely disturbed the purity of African customary values. Thus, an African cultural tradition may, therefore, mean much more than extant traditional practices. Indeed, it may impute a blend of traditional African values, western way of life, and even Asiatic values or traditional practices. See Juma, L. "Reconciling African Customary Law and Human Rights in Kenya: Making a Case for Institutional Reformation and Revitalization of Customary Adjudication Processes." p. 475.

50 Mazrui, Ali. A. "The Re-invention of Africa." pp. 12 and 21.

51 Mazrui, Ali. A. "The Re-invention of Africa." p. 13.

52 Mazrui, Ali. A. "The Re-invention of Africa." p. 76.

53 Mazrui, Ali. A. "The Re-invention of Africa." p. 11.

54 Article 8, *Constitution of Kenya* (2010).

'[t]he Government of the Federation or of a State shall not adopt any religion as State Religion'. And '[U]ganda shall not adopt a State religion'.

The problem with this constitutional uniformity, modelled on a northern power, is that it belies the social, cultural and political disparities. For instance, the insistence on non-entanglement with religion at the constitutional level in Africa might be unrealistic because of the unique requirements of African religion and Islam both critical parties to the triple heritage. It has been shown that African religion permeates nearly all aspects of African life to the extent of making the separation of *faith* from *action* illusory. Practitioners of African religion are known to experience their faith long before birth, throughout life, and way after death. As John Mbiti ably demonstrated,

> [w]here the African is, there is his religion: he carries it to the fields where he is sowing seeds or harvesting a new crop; he takes it with him to the beer party or to attend a funeral ceremony; and if he is educated, he takes religion with him to the examination room at school or in the university; if he is a politician he takes it to the house of parliament.[55]

The point Mbiti makes is that for the Africans, 'the whole of existence is a religious phenomenon', and further that the African is deeply religious in a completely religious universe.[56] In this light, Reuben Musiime rightly concludes that 'Africans cannot truly claim to be agnostic, atheistic, or irreligious'.[57] Because of this, state-religion relations in Africa require to be cast against a backdrop whereby 'belief in the supernatural, and law may be fused and mutually supportive'.[58]

Similarly, Islam has detailed teachings on the state and its functioning and many of its adherents view Islamic law as a complete code which they are

---

55 Mbiti, John. Samuel. *African religions and philosophy*. East African Educational Publishers Ltd, 1969, p. 142.

56 Mbiti, John. Samuel. *African religions and philosophy*.

57 Musiime, Reuben. "A Critical Evaluation of The Religious Education Curriculum for Secondary School Students in Uganda." Dissertation presented to the Graduate Council of the University of North Texas in partial fulfillment of the requirements for the degree of Doctor of Philosophy, December 1996, p. 13.

58 Doren, Van. JW. "African Tradition and Western Common Law: A study in Contradiction." *The SM Otieno case: Death and burial in modern Kenya*, edited by Ojwang. Boma, J. and Mugambi. Ndwiga. J. 1989, p. 128; Tessman, Gunther. "Homosexuality among the Negroes of Cameroon and a Pangwe Tale" *Boy-Wives and Female-Husbands: Studies in African Homosexualities*, edited by Murray. Stephen. Murray. O. and Will. Roscoe, 1998, p. 149.

bound to respect and practice.[59] Less wonder, contemporary proponents of the Islamic state in Africa usually 'seek to use the powers and institutions of the state, as constituted by European colonialism and continued after independence, to coercively regulate individual behaviour and social relations in the specific ways selected by ruling elites'.[60] At the very extreme, fundamentalist Islam regards Shari'a 'as the only legitimate basis for governance', Shari'a being the divinely revealed body of law.[61] Islam is so neatly connected with politics that even Abdullahi An-Na'im, a noteworthy opponent of the Islamic state, accepts Islamic political parties and politics as legitimate even in a secular state setting.[62]

On the other hand, because of the age of the enlightenment, the reformation and related developments, the Western civilisation has evolved to the extent of socialising Christian theology to accept state-secularism.[63] Prior to the 19th century, law's jurisdiction to enforce moral or religious doctrines (in what is now called Europe) was widely acknowledged since church and state[64] were fused. In fact, moral or religious questions in the adjudication of law were hardly controversial mainly because it was possible to appeal to an absolute authority (deity) in case of any disagreement.[65] Koos Malan has written about an era, christened 'Republic Christiana', when 'politics were not state-driven, but in fact a mere branch of theology'.[66] During this period, the maintenance of social and political cohesion was not a function of politics but, rather,

59 Ebeku, Kaniye. "Beyond Terrorism: Boko Haram Attacks and National Constitutional Questions in Nigeria." *Sri Lanka Journal of International Law*, vol. 23, 2011, 16.

60 An-Na'im, Ahmed. A. "Islam, State and Politics: Separate but Interactive." obtained at www.brookings.edu. p. 7.

61 Mara. Pevkin, "The legal Foundation of the Islamic state." *The Brookings Project on the US Relations with the Islamic World*, Analysis Paper, no. 23, July 2016, Center for Middle East Policy. p. 12.

62 An-Na'im, Ahmed. A. "Islam, State and Politics: Separate but Interactive." obtained at www.brookings.edu. p. 5.

63 Sheehan, Jonathan. "Religion, and the Enigma of Secularization: A Review Essay." The *American Historical Review*, vol. 108, no. 4, 2003, pp. 1061–1080.

64 It is acknowledged that the term 'state' might not be completely apt because earlier systems of government did not always respond to the characteristics of the state as it is today known.

65 Bassham, Gregory. "Legislating Morality: Scoring the Hart-Devlin Debate after Fifty years." *Ratio Juris*, vol. 25, 2012, p. 118.

66 Malan, Koos. *Politocracy – An Assessment of the Coercive Logic of the Territorial State.* Pretoria University Law Press, 2012, p. 5.

the province of religion.[67] A key attribute of this era was that membership to the Christian order was considered more significant than loyalty towards the state.[68] This tradition operated for centuries until the intense attacks by influential enlightenment philosophers like Thomas Hobbes (1588–1679),[69] Rene Descartes (1596–1650),[70] John Locke (1632–1704),[71] Baron Montesquieu (1689–1755),[72] Francois-Marie Arouet (otherwise known as Voltaire, 1694–1778), Jean-Jacques Rousseau (1712–1778),[73] and Immanuel Kant (1724–1804).[74] By 1680, 'the ideal of a universal monarchy and a united general Christendom had already foundered to such an extent that it was replaced by the more apt concept of Europe'.[75]

Enlightenment philosophy uprooted authoritarian regimes, dethroned tradition and entrenched religion, and questioned the moral basis for law and politics.[76] The age of enlightenment championed the concept of limited constitutional government based on consent, liberty and equality for all, tolerance of religious diversity, and the separation of church and state. At the core of this revolution was the triumph of reason over tradition. Understandably, therefore, Kant defined 'enlightenment' as man's emergence from his self-imposed nonage;[77] nonage in this context being 'the inability to use one's own under-

67 By 1600, Western Europe was still referred to as Christendom. See Malan. Koos. *Politocracy – An Assessment of the Coercive Logic of the Territorial State*. p. 5.

68 Malan, Koos. *Politocracy – An Assessment of the Coercive Logic of the Territorial State*. p. 5.

69 See, Hobbes, Thomas. *The Leviathan*. 2011.

70 Descartes is the author of great works, some which had great influence on the enlightenment. These include, Discourse on the method, Passion of the soul, and meditations on first philosophy. See, Descartes, Rene. *The Philosophical Works of Descartes*, 1911.

71 See, Locke, John. *The Second Treatise on Government*, 2012.

72 Montesquieu's most influential work is Montesquieu. Baron de la Brede. *The Spirit of Laws*. 1949.

73 See, Rousseau, JJ. *The social contract*. trans M Cranston. 1968.

74 Kant's most influential thoughts on the enlightenment are contained in Kant. I, "What is Enlightenment?" www.columbia.edu/acis/ets/CCREAD/etscc/kant.html. Accessed on 30 September 2020.

75 Malan, Koos. *Politocracy – An Assessment of the Coercive Logic of the Territorial State*. 6.

76 Before the age of reason, 'the cultural horizon of most educated men in western Europe in the early seventeenth century was dominated by two almost unchallenged sources of authority: scripture and the classics ... However great the authority of classical authors, the one unquestionable voice of knowledge and duty was that of God himself, as recorded in the Bible, and particularly in the Old Testament.' Hampson. N. *The enlightenment: An Evaluation of its Assumptions, Attitudes and Values*, 1968, pp. 16–17.

77 Kant, I. "What is Enlightenment?" www.columbia.edu/acis/ets/CCREAD/etscc/kant.html. Accessed on 30 September 2020.

standing without another's guidance.'[78] Kant further posited that only free public use of one's reason can bring enlightenment to mankind.[79] The enlightenment ideals set the stage for public questioning of religion,[80] which before had predominated the state and its political and legal discourse.

Henceforth, there would be efforts to secure the state from the church, to separate the law and morality, and to set the individual free to worship and to enjoy the freedom of conscience.[81] These secular and libertarian reforms came to constitute the 'concept of Europe'.[82] This idea, which is now synonymous with the phenomena of secularisation, sovereign territorial states and religious freedom, represents a major departure from the uniform Christian political order initially in vogue in Europe and parts of Asia. Private persons now only needed to consult their conscience to distinguish right from wrong and not the religious or moral codes.[83] These changes meant that questions which 'before were settled by divine law as pronounced by the churches'[84] were thrown open to debate, even controversy. What the emergent state could competently legislate became subject of argument.[85] It helps to note, however, that the residue of law after the changes above still had significant portions of Christian morality, only that it was articulated in secular terms. It is against this backdrop that Christianity and westernisation, now part of the African cultural trinity, should be understood.

This conceptual framework means that a healthy interaction of the major religions of Africa calls for the establishment of a realistic state-religion regime that is alive to the region's peculiarities. In this regard, the triple heritage lenses are useful in viewing Africa's past and present social, cultural and legal

78 Kant, I. "What is Enlightenment?" www.columbia.edu/acis/ets/CCREAD/etscc/kant.html. Accessed on 30 September 2020.

79 Kant, I. "What is Enlightenment?" www.columbia.edu/acis/ets/CCREAD/etscc/kant.html. Accessed on 30 September 2020.

80 Kant, I. "What is Enlightenment?" www.columbia.edu/acis/ets/CCREAD/etscc/kant.html. Accessed on 30 September 2020.

81 Devlin, P. "Law, Democracy, and Morality." *University of Pennsylvania Law Review*, vol. 110, no. 5, 1962, p. 635.

82 Malan, Koos. *Politocracy – An Assessment of the Coercive Logic of the Territorial State*. p. 6.

83 Devlin, P. "Law, Democracy, and Morality." p. 635.

84 Devlin, P. "Law, Democracy, and Morality." p. 635.

85 However, the ideal of free conscience sometimes tumbled. A case in point is *Rex v Delaval*, whereby as late as 1913, in England, Lord Mansfield still upheld the view that the Court of King's Bench was the custodian of the morals (*custos morum*) of the people and had inherent jurisdiction over offences *contra bonos mores*. See, *Rex v Delaval*, 197 Eng Rep 1913 (KB 1963).

developments. They are useful in explaining the visitation and colonial periods, during which indigenous African values and institutions had significant foreign input. Mazrui's theory also helps explain Africa's post-colonial developments in the light of latter-day cultural paradigms. In the context of state-religion relations, the triple heritage theory helps establish the point that to insist on a religious state or a pure separation between the state and religion in Africa, as some have understood northern secularism to imply, is to denounce the inert character of African polities.

Part 3: African Case Studies in the Secular State Conundrum

I have already stated that policy organs in the African study countries often incorporate the concept of state-secularism in a manner that disadvantages African religion (and sometimes Islam) for the benefit of the Christian faith which has enjoyed privileged status since the pre-colonial missionary days. This misapplication of the concept of state secularism, which has occasioned unfathomable injustices especially to practitioners of African religion, Islam, and other minority religions and unnecessary societal conflicts and unwarranted juridical inconsistencies, arises in the continuation of colonial policies and the haphazard application of northern state-secularism ideals.

In this section, I discuss the practice of state-secularism in the African study countries in relation to their northern counterparts based on three main indicators – whether the state i) subjects religion to its jurisdiction, ii) adopts an identity that is representative of the religious diversity of its people, and iii) formulates policies on objective rather than dogmatic criteria. The aim of this discussion is to show, firstly, that besides subjecting religion to the dictates of the constitution, secular state practice varies greatly meaning that the African study countries have the latitude to adopt the most appropriate policies for their situation, secondly, that none of the northern study countries has succeeded in eliminating religion from the public sphere completely. This finding is invoked below in Part 4, especially in questioning, firstly, the tough resolve in Kenya and Uganda to keep certain aspects of religion out of educational institutions and, secondly, the preferential religious instruction in all the African study countries. And finally, that it is the unique history of the northern secular states rather than any other consideration which informs their practice of secularism, a reality which the African study countries should reckon.

Speaking of the unique history of northern secular states, according to Ahmet Kuru, there are two main strands of state-secularism: assertive and passive secularism.[86] Assertive secularism takes an active role in subordinating religion to the power of the state.[87] It is normal for assertive secular states to undermine certain forms of religious expression in public spaces as in the cases of France and Turkey.[88] This aggressive version of secularism arises in instances where secularists dethrone well-established religious hegemonies usually during the critical juncture.[89] In France and Turkey, 'anticlericalism' among the republican elite emerged as a reaction to well-entrenched ancient regimes based on the marriage of monarchy and hegemonic religion.[90] The architects of assertive secularism in Turkey took charge after overthrowing the Ottoman Empire during the 1923 revolution.[91] Coming from a tradition that fused state and religion, the revolutionaries (led by Kemal Ataturk) sought to fashion Turkey as a modern economy along the lines of Western Europe. Although economic development is normally the active chemical in the metamorphosis of societies founded on traditional, cultural and religious practices into modern civilisations based on logic and science, Turkey's forefathers put the 'cart before the horse'. Without a proper history of industrialisation, urbanisation or modernisation such as had operated in Europe, the Kemalists, once in power, superimposed a Western-style liberal democracy with the concept of state-secularism at the epicentre of the socio-cultural eruption.[92] These changes attained constitutional expression for the first time in 1937[93] and were re-emphasised by the 1982 Constitution.[94] *Laicité*, as French

86 For a discussion on the dichotomy, see, Kuru, AT. "Passive and assertive secularism: Historical conditions, ideological struggles, and state policies towards religion." p. 571.

87 Kuru, AT. "Passive and Assertive Secularism: Historical Conditions, Ideological Struggles, and State Policies towards Religion." p. 571.

88 Kuru, AT. "Passive and Assertive Secularism: Historical Conditions, Ideological Struggles, and State Policies towards Religion." p. 571.

89 '[C]ritical junctures are moments of relative structural indeterminism when wilful actors shape outcomes in a more voluntary fashion than normal circumstances permit ... Before a critical juncture, a broad range of outcomes is possible; after a critical juncture, enduring institutions and structures are created, and the range of possible outcomes is narrowed considerably.' See Mahoney, J. *The Legacies of Liberalism: Path Dependence and Political Regimes in Central America.* 2001, p. 7, as cited in Kuru, AT. "Passive and Assertive Secularism: Historical Conditions, Ideological Struggles, and State Policies towards Religion." p. 585.

90 Kuru, AT. *Secularism and State Policies toward Religion.* p. 14.

91 Kuru, AT. *Secularism and State Policies toward Religion.* pp. 14, 27, 163–164.

92 Kuru, AT. *Secularism and State Policies toward Religion.* 18.

93 Adanali, A.H. "The Presidency of Religious Affairs and the Principle of Secularism in Turkey." *The Muslim World*, vol. 98, 2008, 228.

94 The Constitution was adopted by the Constituent Assembly on 18 October 1982 to be submitted to referendum and published in the Official Gazette dated 20 October 1982 and numbered 17844; republished in the repeating Official Gazette dated 9 November 1982 and

secularism is known, emerged from turbulent struggles between Government and the Church, which date back to the 1789 revolution.[95] The contests culminated in the confiscation of church property between 1901 and 1905 in an effort to separate the 'temporal' from the 'eternal'. It is the antagonistic relations between the republicans and the religious institutions that gave rise to assertive secularism.[96]

On the flip side of the coin that is assertive secularism is the passive strand, which leaves sufficient latitude for public manifestation of religion.[97] A state ends up adopting the passive model where at the point of its founding there is no predominant state-religion to be deposed.[98] There being no established 'caliphate' or 'theocracy', it is normally possible for such a state to negotiate concessions both for religious freedom and secular governance. A case in point is the US, which emerged as 'a new country of immigrants that lacked an ancient regime.'[99] The exodus to America was partly 'to escape the bondage of laws which compelled them to support and attend government favoured churches'.[100] This, and the fact that the old European tendencies of erecting religious establishments that mandated compulsory payment of tithes and taxes by both believers and non-believers had begun to take root in the new America,[101] enabled the competing secular and religious interests to achieve

numbered 17863 in the aftermath of its submission to referendum on 7 November 1982 (Act No. 2709).

95 Kuru, AT. "Passive and Assertive Secularism: Historical Conditions, Ideological Struggles, and State Policies towards Religion." p. 572. Also, Keddie, NR. "Secularism and its Discontents." *Daedalus on Secularism and Religion*, vol. 132, no. 3, 2003, pp. 14, 18. Also, Gunn T.J. "French Secularism as Utopia and Myth." *Houston Law Review*, vol. 42, no. 1, 2005, p. 82.

96 Kuru, AT. "Passive and Assertive Secularism: Historical Conditions, Ideological Struggles, and State Policies towards Religion." p. 572.

97 Kuru, AT. "Passive and Assertive Secularism: Historical Conditions, Ideological Struggles, and State Policies towards Religion." p. 571.

98 Kuru, AT. "Passive and Assertive Secularism: Historical Conditions, Ideological Struggles, and State Policies towards Religion." p. 570.

99 Kuru, AT. "Passive and Assertive Secularism: Historical Conditions, Ideological Struggles, and State Policies towards Religion." p. 572.

100 For a summary of the history of secularism in the new America, see, *Everson v Board of Education of Ewing TP et al.* No 52. Decided on 19 February 1947.

101 In *Everson v Board of Education of Ewing TP et al*, it is stated: 'These practices of the old world were transplanted to and began to thrive in the soil of the new America. The very charters granted to the individuals and companies designated to make the laws which would control the destinies of the colonials authorised these individuals and companies to erect religious establishments which all, whether believers or non-believers, would be required to support and attend.'

a consensus on the separation of church and state at the federal level.[102] It is arguable that, like the US, the African study countries were predestined to adopt passive secularism for the reason that the entities as are today known are creations of the colonial epoch[103] and the invented territories had no major or wholesome historical experience with compulsive religious establishments.[104] This could be why the African study countries exhibit 'a far greater acceptance of state involvement with religious affairs' than their European counterparts.[105] However, as this contribution shows, the practice of the African study countries does not always respond to their unique historical requirements.

3.1 *The Status of Religion in the Constitutional State*

In all the case studies I review, the secular order subjects religion to the power of the state through the devices of a supreme constitution and a sovereign people or nation. The principle of constitutional supremacy, which places the constitutional document at a hierarchical vantage point, enabling it to triumph over religion and all other norms, has juridical origins in the landmark precedent of the Supreme Court of the US, *Marbury v Madison.*[106] In this decision, the US Supreme Court found that the Constitution, being the main source of law, is paramount and is to prevail where an alternative or conflicting position is provided for in any other law obviously including religious or customary law. The US Supreme Court substantiated that a constitution is

102 Kuru, AT. "Passive and Assertive Secularism: Historical Conditions, Ideological Struggles, and State Policies towards Religion." p. 572. As Justice Frankfurter observed in *People of State of Illinois ex rel. McCollum v Board of Education of School District No 71, Champaign County, Illinois, et al* 68 (Supreme Court 461), 'Zealous watchfulness against fusion of secular and religious activities by Government itself, through any of its instruments but especially through its educational agencies, was the democratic response of the American community to the particular needs of a young and growing nation, unique in the composition of its people.'

103 Even the political entities themselves were only patched together by colonial administrators. For instance, the colony of Lagos and the two protectorates were only amalgamated in 1914 into the entity that is now known as Nigeria. Nmehielle, VO. "Sharia Law in the Northern States of Nigeria: To implement or not to Implement, the Constitutionality is the Question." *Human Rights Quarterly*, vol. 26, 2004, p. 734.

104 Nmehielle, VO. "Sharia Law in The Northern States of Nigeria: To Implement or not to Implement, the Constitutionality is the Question." p. 734. However, certain regions under these territories were before colonialism ruled by religious establishments. A case in point is the East African Coastal strip which was governed by the Sultan of Zanzibar using sharia. A similar situation obtained in parts of Northern Nigeria where concrete 'caliphates' existed.

105 Hackett. RIJ. "Regulating Religious Freedom in Africa." *Emory International Law Review*, vol. 25, 2011, p. 860.

106 *Marbury v Madison* (1803), The Supreme Court of the United States.

written to limit government a role that is served best where all other rules are subordinated by it.

Turkey's Constitution enunciates this principle by providing that 'the provisions of the Constitution are fundamental legal rules binding upon legislative, executive and judicial organs, and administrative authorities and other institutions and individuals' and further that 'laws shall not be contrary to the Constitution'.[107]

The *Marbury* principle almost immediately found its way into the precincts of African courts on attainment of self-government and its influence remains alive. Within a decade of independence, the High Court of Kenya in *Okunda v Republic*[108] concluded that supremacy of the Constitution was a most visible characteristic of the Constitution noting that

> [i]f a constitutional lawyer were to write about in the same strain as Dicey did about England, he would, to be accurate, have to emphasize the supremacy of the constitution rather than one organ of government. The Constitution and any Acts amending it must in the nature of things override all other laws.[109]

This constitutional principle is maintained in Kenya's 2010 Constitution as well as in Nigeria and Uganda. The first substantive Article of the Constitution of Nigeria provides:

> (1) This Constitution is supreme and its provisions shall have binding force on the authorities and persons throughout the Federal Republic of Nigeria.
>
> (2) The Federal Republic of Nigeria shall not be governed, nor shall any persons or group of persons take control of the Government of Nigeria or any part thereof, except in accordance with the provisions of this Constitution.

---

107 Article 11, *The Constitution of the Republic of Turkey* (1982).

108 *Okunda v Republic*, (1970) EA, pp. 453.

109 The Court had in mind section 3 of Kenya's repealed Constitution which provided: 'This Constitution is the Constitution of the Republic of Kenya and shall have the force of law throughout Kenya and, subject to section 47, if any other law is inconsistent with this Constitution, this Constitution shall prevail and the other law shall, to the extent of the inconsistency, be void.' Other precedents that have explored the principle of constitutional supremacy include *Stephen Mwai Gachiengo and Albert Muthee Kahuhia v Republic of Kenya* (Nairobi High Court Criminal Application No. 302 of 2000); *Kenya Bankers Association & Others v Minister of Finance and Another* (2002) KLR 61; and *Jesse Kamau & 25 Others v Attorney General*, (2010) eKLR.

> (3) If any other law is inconsistent with the provisions of this Constitution, this Constitution shall prevail, and that other law shall, to the extent of the inconsistency, be void.[110]

Uganda's Constitution similarly stamps its authority in the following terms:

> (1) This Constitution is the supreme law of Uganda and shall have binding force on all authorities and persons throughout Uganda.
>
> (2) If any other law or any custom is inconsistent with any of the provisions of this Constitution, the Constitution shall prevail, and that other law or custom shall, to the extent of the inconsistency, be void.[111]

In addition to declaring themselves supreme, the constitutions of France,[112] Kenya[113] and Uganda[114] acknowledge the sovereignty of the people. In France, national sovereignty is vested in the people who are required to exercise this power through their representatives and by means of referendum.[115] In view of this, France declares itself a Government of the people, governed by the people and for the people.[116] In Kenya and Uganda, sovereign power is vested in the people who may exercise this mandate either directly or through democratically elected representatives.[117] A sovereign people are ultimate in that they have the power to constitute the frame of their government, to choose those to run such government, and to be involved in governing.[118] In Turkey, sovereignty belongs to the nation as an entity.[119]

Through supreme constitutions and sovereign people or nations, the constitutions of the African case studies have exerted their influence over other

110 Article 1, *Constitution of Nigeria* (1999).

111 Article 2, *Constitution of Uganda* (1995).

112 Article 3, *Constitution of France* (4 October 1958). It is trite that 'the principles enshrined in the Constitution are considered to have a value superior to general legislation.' See, Troper, M. "French Secularism, or Laicité." *Cardozo Law Review*, vol. 21, 1999–2000, p. 1280.

113 Article 1, Constitution of Kenya (2010).

114 Article 1, Constitution of Uganda (1995).

115 Article 3, Constitution of France (4 October 1958).

116 Article 2, Constitution of France (4 October 1958).

117 Article 1, *Constitution of Kenya* (2010) and Uganda (1995).

118 Nwabueze, BO. *Presidentialism in Commonwealth Africa*. 1974, p. 292.

119 Article 6, *Constitution of Turkey* (4 October 1958).

competing comprehensive doctrines,[120] including religion, just like their northern counterparts.

3.2 *Constitutional Expression of Secularity*

All the study countries indicate their intention to abide by secular principles at the constitutional level.[121] The constitutions articulate this statement in two broad ways; expressly or by providing against the establishment of state religion. In the first category fall France and Turkey which declare the secular credentials of their constitutions overtly. The latter category has the constitutions of the US, Kenya, Nigeria, and Uganda, which merely provide against the establishment of state religion(s).

3.2.1 The Express Secular Statement Model

France and Turkey articulate their secular credentials expressly. The notion of secularism in France was initially articulated in the French Law of 1905 through the guarantee of 'the liberty of conscience' and the 'free exercise of religion, under restrictions prescribed by the interest in public order'.[122] This legislation also prevented the State from recognising, remunerating, or subsidising any religious denomination.[123] Later, in October 1958, France promulgated a new Constitution, which legitimises the secular tradition further by stipulating that

---

120 By 'comprehensive doctrines', John Rawls meant principles that '[i]nclude conceptions of what is of value in human life, and ideals of personal character, as well as ideals of friendship and of familial and associational relationships, and much else that is to inform our conduct, and in the limit to our life as a whole.' J Rawls *Political liberalism* (2005) xvii. Although religious conceptions are clear examples of comprehensive doctrines, they are not the only ones. Baxter (n 298 above) p. 1340.

121 It is instructive that the legal declaration of secular status does not necessarily mean the practice will follow the law. In Turkey, for instance, despite secular reforms in the area of family law, this has not translated into comprehensive changes. Unofficial religious laws continue to operate among the people. See, for instance, Yilmaz, Ihsan. "Secular Law and the Emergence of Unofficial Turkish Islamic Law." *The Middle East Journal*, vol. 56, no. 1, 2002, pp. 113–131.

122 Article 1, Law of December 1905. However, it is important to note that state-religion relations in France have a long history dating back to the 1631 Treaty of Rights and Freedoms of the Gallican Church which *inter alia* enunciated the following principles: "The temporal power is distinct from the spiritual power and is independent of it; the pope cannot legislate for the king; the king can exercise surveillance over religious orders (…); and, finally, the king can intervene in doctrinal matters, as he did, for example, in the Jansenist affair" – See Troper, M. "French Secularism, or Laicité." p. 1273.

123 Article 2, Law of December 1905.

the State 'shall be an indivisible, *secular*, democratic and social Republic'.[124] The 1958 Constitution also carries the promise to ensure the equality of all citizens before the law, without distinction of origin, race or religion and to respect all beliefs.[125]

Turkey's Constitution conveys the Kemal Atatürk revolution's[126] desire that 'sacred religious feelings shall not be involved in State affairs and politics as required by the principles of secularism' emphatically.[127] In furtherance of this preambular inspiration, Article 2 of the Constitution identifies secularism as one of the distinguishing characteristics of the legal system. It states:

> The Republic of Turkey is a democratic, secular [*laik*] and social state governed by the rule of law, within the notions of public peace, national solidarity and justice, respecting human rights, loyal to the nationalism of Ataturk, and based on the fundamental tenets set forth in the preamble.

The centrality of secularism in Turkey is additionally manifested by Article 174 of the Constitution which declares invalid, *a priori*, any interpretation of the supreme law that contradicts a set of revolutionary legislations aimed at raising the Turkish society above the level of contemporary civilisation and safeguarding the secular character of the Republic.[128] In an unequivocal and unambiguous manner, France and Turkey declare their secularity.

3.2.2 The Anti-Establishment Model

Unlike France and Turkey, the constitutions of the US, Kenya, Nigeria and Uganda are silent on their secular characteristics. Without indicating whether

---

124 Article 1, *Constitution of France* (1958). Emphasis added.

125 Article 1, *Constitution of France* (1958).

126 Mustafa Kemal Ataturk led Turkish troops in repelling European invaders hence securing an independent Turkey. For a discussion on this conquest, see Keddie, NR. "Secularism and its Discontents." *Daedalus on Secularism and Religion*, vol. 32, no. 3, p. 3. The Ataturk revolution aimed at creating a modern nation that is religiously homogenous. See, Shively. Kim. "Religious Bodies and the Secular State: The Merve Kavakci Affair." *Journal of Middle East Women's Studies*, vol. 1, no. 3, 2005, 46–72, 54.

127 Preambular Paragraph 5, Constitution of Turkey. Published in official Gazette dated on 9 November 1982. Act No 2709.

128 The laws which the Constitution raises above the power of review of courts include: Act No 430 of 3 March 1925 (1340) on the unification of the educational system; Act No 671 of 25 November 1925 (1341) on the wearing of hats; Act No 677 of 30 November 1925 (1341) on the closure of dervish monasteries and tombs, the abolition of the Office of Keeper of Tombs and the abolition and prohibition of certain titles; the principle of civil marriage adopted with the Turkish Civil Code No 743 of 17 February 1926 and article 110 of the Code; Act No 2590 of 26 November 1934 on the abolitions of certain titles and appellations; and Act No 2596 of 3 December 1934 on the prohibition of the wearing of certain garments.

the State is secular, religious or anti-religious, the US First Amendment[129] merely prevents Congress from making any law respecting an establishment of religion, or prohibiting the free exercise thereof. Initially, this provision only concerned Congress. However, with the ratification of the Fourteenth Amendment, state legislatures were enjoined to the principle against establishment of religion and the guarantee of the exercise of religious freedom.[130]

In the absence of further constitutional specifications, the US Supreme Court has moved to give some flesh to the quite skeletal 'Establishment Clause'. According to this jurisprudence, the Establishment Clause was intended to exorcise three main demons: first, the active involvement of the State(s) in religious activities; second, state-sponsorship of religion and, third, financial support of religious institutions or programmes.[131] The US Supreme Court understands the Constitution to mean that no government in the US can either set up a church or pass laws which aid any religion, or prefer one religion over another.[132] Public resources may also not be used to support any religious activities or institutions.[133] Additionally, both levels of Government are estopped from participating in the affairs of any religious organisations or groups and *vice versa*.[134]

Against this backdrop, it is clear that the US has systematically entrenched a belief that 'if nowhere else, in the relation between church and State, "good fences make good neighbours"'.[135] The premise upon which this notion rests is that 'both religion and government can best work to achieve their lofty aims if each is left free from the other within its respective sphere'[136] and the State is established for secular purposes; never entangling itself with, advancing or inhibiting religion.[137] As Justice Hugo Black concluded, in *Everson v Board*

129 Amendment 1 – Freedom of Religion, Press, Expression. Ratified 15 December 1791.

130 The Fourteenth Amendment was passed by Congress on 13 June 1866; and ratified on 9 July 1868. Section 1 of the Amendment reads: 'No state shall make or enforce any law which shall abridge the privileges or immunities of citizens of the United States; nor shall any state deprive any liberty without due process of law; nor deny to any person within its jurisdiction the equal protection of the laws.'

131 *Lemon v Kurtzman* (1971) Supreme Court of the United States, p. 2111.

132 *Everson v Board of Education of Ewing TP et al*, (1947) Supreme Court of the United States, 504, at pp. 511 and 512.

133 *Everson v Board of Education of Ewing TP et al*, at pp. 511 and 512.

134 *Everson v Board of Education of Ewing TP et al*, at pp. 511 and 512.

135 *People of State of Illinois v Board of Education*. As per Frankfurter.

136 *People of State of Illinois v Board of Education*, at p. 465. As per Black.

137 *Lemon v Kurtzman*. As per Burger, p. 2111.

of Education of Ewing TP et al, 'the First Amendment erected a wall between church and State which must be kept high and impregnable.'[138]

The African study countries emulate the US formulation of secularism. Although Kenya, Nigeria and Uganda are usually classified as secular states (like in the case of the US), their constitutions shy away from explicitly declaring this status.[139] No single constitutional provision declares the secularity of these legal systems expressly. Rather, the three constitutions merely prohibit the adoption of state religion(s).[140]

Only one statement conveys the state-religion relationship in Kenya, simply that 'there shall be no State religion'.[141] In practice, this provision has been held to incorporate secularism in Kenya's constitutional order. According to the High Court of Kenya, Article 8 of the Constitution boldly and in no uncertain terms makes Kenya a secular State.[142] It also means that 'no religion shall have prevalence over any other and no particular one should be seen as the one each citizen should follow'.[143] It may however, be argued that the brevity of the 'anti-establishment statement' is wanting particularly when it is considered that earlier draft constitutions contained more elaborate provisions on the aspect.

The Draft Constitution of Kenya, 2004 (Bomas Draft),[144] stated, firstly, that State and religion would be separate,[145] secondly, that there would be no State religion,[146] and, finally, that the State would treat all religions equally.[147] The omission of the first and last provisions from the 2010 Constitution therefore

---

138 *Everson v Board of Education of Ewing TP* at p. 513.

139 As per the State-Religion Regimes Index of 197 Countries, Kenya, Uganda and Nigeria are secular states. See, Kuru, AT. *Secularism and State Policies toward Religion*. p. 253.

140 Article 8, *Constitution of Kenya* (2010); Section 10, *Constitution of Nigeria* (1999), and Section 7, *Constitution of Uganda* (1995).

141 Article 8, *Constitution of Kenya* (2010). Article 8 is a significant improvement from the position in the repealed Constitution which did not expressly provide that Kenya is a secular state; did not provide for a State religion; and did not overtly provide that the church would be separate from religion. See, Mujuzi, JD. "Separating the Church from State: The Kenyan High Court's Decision in *Jesse Kamau and 25 others v Attorney General*." *Journal of African Law*, vol. 2, 2011, p. 317.

142 *Republic v the Head Teacher, Kenya High School & Another, ex parte SMY*, [2012] eKLR.

143 [2014] eKLR. Petition No 431 of 2012 between Seventh Day Adventist Church (East Africa) Limited and the Minister for Education (1st Respondent); Attorney General (2nd Respondent); Board of Governors Alliance High School (Interested Party); and National Gender and Equality Commission (Amicus Curiae). para. 48.

144 Adopted by the National Constitution Conference on 15 March 2004.

145 Article 9(1), Draft Constitution of Kenya 2004.

146 Article 9(2), Draft Constitution of Kenya 2004.

147 Article 9(3), Draft Constitution of Kenya 2004.

leaves a lot to be desired. It not only re-ignites a general debate around the relationship between State and religion; the ultimate exclusion of the two critical details from the 'secularity statement' also signals that the new order might not be designed to respect the tenets of state-secularism fully. In reaction to the redacted statement on religion in the 2010 Constitution, a section of the Christian community has not hidden its suspicion that the elimination of detailed stipulations on the secular identity of the legal system is meant to herald an influential role for the State in the running of Islamic religious courts.[148] The Christians appear to read from Rosalind Hackett's view that African states "prefer the designation of 'multi-religious' rather than 'secular' states"[149] to accommodate 'Muslim suspicion of the Western underpinnings of secularism', and the 'more general conviction that morality is closely tied to religious commitment'.[150]

Like the US and Kenya, the 1999 Constitution of Nigeria forbids the Federal and all state governments from adopting any religious tradition.[151] Beyond this statement, the Constitution says nothing else regarding the secularity of the State and neither does it give directions on the genre of state-religion relations it envisions. Varied interpretations of Nigeria's secularism have been attempted. One side of the argument goes that Article 10 makes Nigeria a secular state.[152] It is claimed, on the other side, that in spite of this Article, 'Nigeria is not a secular state and religion has a place in Nigerian public life'.[153] Mansur Noibi, Enyinna Nwauche and Is-haq Oloyede belong to the latter school. According to Noibi, Nigeria is a multi-religious state (predominated by Islam and Christianity) which does not prevent the Federal Government or any state government from associating or identifying with any religion as long as this

148 Vanderpoel, RS. "Religious Equity in Kenya? Adjudicating the Constitutionality of Kenya's Kadhis' courts." www.religionanddiversity.ca. Accessed 27 November 2014.

149 Hackett, RIJ. "Regulating Religious Freedom in Africa." *Emory International Law Review*, vol. 25, 2011, p. 860.

150 Hackett, RIJ. "Regulating Religious Freedom in Africa." p. 860.

151 Section 10, 1999 Constitution of Nigeria.

152 See, Nwauche, Enyinna. S. "Law, Religion and Human Rights in Nigeria." *African Human Rights Law Journal*, vol. 2, no. 8, 2008, p. 572.

153 See, Nwauche, Enyinna. S. "Law, Religion and Human Rights in Nigeria." p. 572. In another context it has been written: 'The status of Nigeria *vis a vis* religion is still a subject of contestation, argument and intellectual discussions.' See, Oloyede, I. Egbewole W. & Oloyede, H. "The operational complexities of "free exercise" and "adoption of religion" clauses in the Nigerian Constitution." presented at the 2015 Religious Freedom and Religious Pluralism in Africa: Prospects and Limitations Conference.

stops short of an 'adoption'.[154] Commenting on law, religion and human rights in Nigeria, Nwauche agreed with Noibi that

> [o]ur religious demography ... shows that the dominant religions in Nigeria are Islam and Christianity. Their dominance is reinforced by the fact that governments in Nigeria actively promote, sponsor and sustain both religions ... then Nigeria has a state religion(s).[155]

Oloyede likewise contends that Nigeria supports all religious groups and activities to varying degrees, depending on who is in the majority or in power making it a multi-religious rather than a secular state.[156] However, according to Osita Ogbu, secularism is neither opposed nor indifferent to religion since secular states are entitled to seek the creation of a favourable environment for the exercise of religious freedom. Therefore, while some secular states may insist on not intervening in religious affairs with near-rigidity, a state is no less secular because it provides facilities for religious life without discrimination in favour or against any religion.[157] Thus understood, Nigeria is a liberal secular dispensation under which there is no official religion although there is constitutional obligation for the State to facilitate religious life. Nigeria is therefore a secular state formally by the tenor of Article 10 even though Islam and Christianity dominate it functionally.

Not much debate exists in Uganda on the state-religion relations and the non-establishment clause in the Constitution has largely gone untested – unlike Kenya and Nigeria. This could be because Christianity dominates the country and Islam has both fewer converts and a shorter history there.[158]

---

154 Noibi, M., "Shari'a and the Nigerian Constitution – The Jurisdiction of the Shari'a Court of Appeal (2003–2004)." *Year Book of Islamic and Middle East Law Online*, 2003, p. 97.

155 Nwauche has recognised this argument. See, Nwauche, Enyinna. S. "Law, Religion and Human Rights in Nigeria." p. 573.

156 Oloyede, I, Egbewole, W. and Oloyede, H. "The operational complexities of "free exercise" and "adoption of religion" clauses in the Nigerian Constitution."

157 Ogbu, ON. "Is Nigeria a secular state? Law, Human Rights and Religion in Context." p. 156.

158 According to Manisuli Ssenyonjo, by 2008, "Uganda's population numbered approximately 31.3 million, of which approximately 85 percent were Christians, while Muslims represented approximately 12 percent. The balance of the population espoused a variety of other beliefs and convictions, including traditional indigenous religions, Hinduism, the Baha'i faith, Judaism, and atheism, all of which are also practiced freely." Ssenyonjo, Manisuli. "Limits on the Freedom to Manifest one's Religion in Educational Institutions in Uganda and the United Kingdom." *International Journal of Constitutional Law*, vol. 7, no. 2, 2009, pp. 275–305, p. 305.

The Kenyan and Nigerian cases show that for the African study countries, the US anti-establishment model is a more convenient way of declaring their secular identity while at the same time leaving room for adaptability of government policies to the practical realities which entail accommodating certain requirements of the dominant religions. Ideally, this should have enabled the African study countries to both keep the spirit of secularism alive while enabling their governance institutions to flexibly navigate the complex state-religion interactions on case by case basis. But as Part 4 below shows, this has not been the case.

3.3 *State-Identity through National Emblems*

It is possible to glean the study countries' treatment of religion from their state emblems and other symbols such as the preamble, national anthem, official prayer and oath of office. There seems to be a general acceptance that some religious content in state emblems is useful in inspiring the national psyche, stimulating the peoples' commitment and loyalty, and avowing fidelity of government officials to integrity and the rule of law, among other motivational ends. That said, France and Turkey take stricter measures to exclude religion from their state emblems compared to the other study countries. One could therefore talk of religious and areligious emblems.

3.3.1 Religious Emblems

Preambular provisions of the constitutions of Kenya, Nigeria and Uganda proceed from a religious vantage point. In Kenya, the people begin by acknowledging the supremacy of *Almighty God of all creation*[159] before asking Him (God) to bless their country.[160] In the same vein, the people of Uganda dedicate the Constitution for *God* and the country[161] as their counterparts in Nigeria 'firmly and solemnly resolve, to live in unity and harmony as one indivisible and indissoluble sovereign nation under *God*.'[162]

Kenya's National Anthem takes the form of prayer or supplication to '*God of all creation*' whom the people beseech to *bless* the land and nation.[163] In like manner, the people of Nigeria call on the same '*God of creation*', to direct their noble cause, to guide their leaders' right, to help their youth to know the truth and grow in love and honesty, to attain heights by living justly and truthfully

159 Preambular paragraph 1, *Constitution of Kenya* (2010).
160 See, concluding statement of the Preamble, *Constitution of Kenya* (2010).
161 See, concluding statement of the Preamble, *Constitution of Kenya* (2010).
162 Preambular paragraph 2, *Constitution of Kenya* (2010) Emphasis added.
163 Second Schedule, *Constitution of Kenya* (2010).

and to build a nation where peace and justice reigns.[164] In addition to this, Nigerians' pledge to be faithful, loyal and honest, to serve their country with all strength, to defend its unity, and uphold its honour and glory, ends with the phrase '*so help me God*'.[165] Uganda's National Anthem adopts the same 'theology' of invocation by asking '*God*' to uphold the nation as well as secure its destiny in *His* hands.

Besides invoking the name of 'God' in the state emblems discussed above, Kenya's and Uganda's constitutions give high ranking government officials[166] taking oaths of office the option of doing so in the name of a religious deity, the '*Almighty God*,'[167] and crowning such noble undertakings with the prayer '*so help me God*'.[168] Although officials of similar status in Nigeria do not have to invoke the name of the Almighty God in their actual oaths, their vows are prescribed to sign off with the supplication, '*so help me God*'.[169]

There is also an established tradition whereby a standard word of prayer initiates the commencement of parliamentary business in both Kenya and Uganda. Both Houses of Parliament in Kenya (National Assembly and Senate) and the National Assembly of Uganda start business by reciting an almost identical prayer that reads as follows:

> Almighty God, who in Your wisdom and goodness have appointed the offices of Leaders and Parliaments for the welfare of society and the just government of the people, we beseech You to behold with Your abundant favour, us Your servants, whom You have been pleased to call to the performance of important trusts in this Republic. Let Your blessings descend upon us here assembled, and grant that we treat and consider all matters

164 "National Anthem, Nigeria." http://www.nigeriagalleria.com/Nigeria/National-Anthems-Pledge.html. Accessed 30 September 2020.

165 "National Anthem, Nigeria." http://www.nigeriagalleria.com/Nigeria/National-Anthems-Pledge.html. Accessed 30 September 2020.

166 In Kenya, the oaths apply to the following State offices: President; Deputy/Acting President; Speaker/Deputy Speaker National Assembly/Senate; Chief Justice; judges; Cabinet and principal secretaries; and Members of Parliament. In Uganda, the officers to whom the prescribed oaths apply include: President; Deputy President; judges; Speaker of Parliament; Members of Parliament; and Ministers.

167 Third Schedule, *Constitution of Kenya* (2010); also Fourth Schedule, *Constitution of Uganda* (1995).

168 Third Schedule, *Constitution of Kenya* (2010); also Fourth Schedule, *Constitution of Uganda* (1995).

169 Seventh Schedule, *Constitution of Nigeria* (1999). The offices whose oaths are stated in the Seventh Schedule are: President; Governor of a State; Vice President; Deputy Governor; Minister; Commissioner of Special Adviser.

> that shall come under our deliberation in so just and faithful a manner as to promote Your Honour and Glory, and to advance the peace, prosperity and welfare of our Country and of those whose interests You have committed to our charge. AMEN.[170]

In its most significant documents such as the 1776 Declaration of Independence and the National Anthem, the US retains both subtle and express references to the deity. In the former proclamation, America's forefathers appeal to '*the Supreme Judge of the world*' for the rectitude of their intentions and acknowledge the existence of a 'Creator' who endows *His* people with unalienable rights. The latter document establishes the national motto: *In God we Trust*. Although the oath of office for the US President avoids religious sentiments, it is traditionally executed by placing the deponent's hand on the Bible.[171] This aside, school children in the US can no longer recite a pledge that refers to a 'monotheistic God' because such has been held to violate the First Amendment and to have a coercive effect upon children.[172]

3.3.2 Areligious Emblems

In contrast, France and Turkey assert their secularity in most state emblems. France's strict secular ideology has ensured that there is 'no prayer, reference to God, or oaths putting hands on the Bible' in public institutions.[173] Not even constitutional preambular provisions refer to God as is common practice elsewhere. However, the Declaration of the Rights of Man and the Citizen, promulgated before France's secular culture, defers to 'the Supreme Being'[174] and

---

170 As adopted by the National Assembly on 9th January, 2013 during the Fourth Session of the Tenth Parliament and amended during the First Session of the Eleventh Parliament. See Rule 2, 24 of the Rules of Procedure of the Parliament of Uganda for the prayer uttered in the National Assembly of Uganda.

171 The Oath reads as follows: 'I do solemnly swear (or affirm) that I will faithfully execute the office of President of the United States, and will to the best of my ability, preserve, protect, and defend the Constitution of the United States.' *The Presidential Oath of Office*. http://www.infoplease.com/ipa/A0878064.html#ixzz3a6IEMT3R. Accessed 30 September 2020.

172 In *Newdow v US Congress* (328 F.3d 466, 9th Cir. 2003), the United States Court of Appeals, Ninth Circuit, outlawed a statutory pledge which read as follows: 'I pledge allegiance to the Flag of the United States of America, and to the Republic for which it stands, one nation under God, indivisible, with liberty and justice for all'. The Court argued that 'a profession that we are a nation 'under God' is identical, for Establishment Clause purposes, to a profession that we are a nation 'under Jesus,' a nation 'under Vishnu.' A nation 'under Zeus,' or a nation 'under no god.'"

173 Kuru, AT. *Secularism and State Policies toward Religion*. p. 109.

174 See, Preamble, Declaration of the Rights of Man and the Citizen (1789).

the National Anthem, *La Marseillaise*, makes a very casual reference to the 'Good Lord'.

Rather than draw inspiration from a religious deity, the preamble of Turkey's Constitution highlights that 'sacred religious feelings shall absolutely not be involved in state affairs and politics as required by the principle of secularism'.[175] The same philosophy is evident in the prescribed oath of office for Members of the Grand National Assembly, which requires deponents to affirm 'the supremacy of law, the democratic and secular republic, and the principles and reforms of Atatürk'.[176] The President of Turkey also swears 'to abide by the Constitution, the rule of law, democracy, the principles and reforms of Atatürk, and the principles of the secular republic'.[177] The exception however, is the National Anthem, which makes several references to God.

A fair conclusion for this section is to say that none of the study countries is successful in keeping state emblems pure although in France and Turkey the success rate is far higher.

3.4 *Secularism and Foundation of State Policies*

Through exploring whether the study countries i) commit state-resources to support religious institutions and activities, and ii) permit the politicisation of religion, this section assesses the neutrality of the states' policies, programmes and politics, and the extent of disentanglement with religious institutions and activities. I show that state practice on these aspects varies greatly, and no study country has managed to contain public manifestation of religion.

3.4.1 State-Secularism and Support for Religious Institutions and Activities

While it is normally thought that secular states are ardent at divorcing the temporal from the spiritual, the experience of the study countries exhibits both approaches. On one end are secular states like France, Turkey, Kenya and Nigeria, which intercede in religious affairs through funding and other policy interventions; on the other, is the US with the policy of non-entanglement in religious programmes.

175 See, Preambular para 5, *Constitution of Turkey* (1982).

176 Article 81, *Constitution of Turkey* (1982).

177 Article 103, *Constitution of Turkey* (1982).

3.4.1.1 *The Entanglement Policy*

Although classified as assertive secular dispensations, France and Turkey extend support for certain religious activities. The same scenario applies to passive secular countries in Africa, Kenya and Nigeria.

France supports a number of religious activities both within and without its territorial jurisdiction. For example, it subsidises religious (mainly Catholic) schools that agree to admit students from all faiths and teach the secular national curriculum.[178] Since the revolutions of early 1900s when 'secularists' ousted 'religionists' and dispossessed them of buildings and other assets, the French Government funds the maintenance of thousands of churches and synagogues.[179] These premises were not transferred back to religious institutions, and the State had to devise a means of putting them at the churches' disposal, which implied the need for a highly complex legal system for determining the terms of their use and upkeep.[180] Still, in 1920, the Government of France was involved in the construction of the earliest Mosque in the country, the Paris Mosque, using public resources.[181] This time, a secular explanation for the expenditure was given as to honour Muslim soldiers who fought alongside France in the Great War of 1914–18.[182] Further, in the region of Alsace-Moselle[183] and some overseas colonies such as Guyana, which are exempted from the State's secular policies, the French Government supports religion by meeting the salaries of the clergy.[184]

The same accommodative philosophy applies in Turkey, which despite commitment to the assertive version of secularism expends significant public resources on aspects of the Islamic faith. Through the Directorate of Religious Affairs (DRA), the Turkish State recruits, trains and maintains preachers (*Imams*) at public expense.[185] It also holds regular conferences aimed at seek-

178 Kuru, AT. *Secularism and State Policies toward Religion.* p. 109.

179 Kuru, AT. *Secularism and State Policies toward Religion.* p. 12.

180 Troper, M. "French Secularism, or Laicité." p. 1277.

181 Gunn (n 45 above) p. 89.

182 See, Troper, M. "French Secularism, or Laicité." p. 1279.

183 Alsace-Moselle comprises three departments which had been incorporated into Germany after France was defeated in 1871. However, the territories became French again after the First World War. Since the region was not part of France during the writing of the Law of 1905, it is normally exempted from the secular principles of State. See, Troper, M. "French Secularism, or Laicité." p. 1278.

184 Kuru, AT. *Secularism and State Policies toward Religion.* p. 111. The French State pays mainly Catholic, Lutheran, Calvin and Judaist clergy in Alsace-Moselle, and Catholic clergy in Guyana.

185 See, Adanali, AH. "The Presidency of Religious Affairs and the Principle of Secularism in Turkey." The Muslim World, vol. 98, 2008, p. 229. Toprak, B. "Islam and the Secular State in

ing consensus on various doctrinal items, and controls the content of the sermons delivered at the various religious platforms in the country. In other words, there exists in Turkey an elaborate State-supported 'religious public service' whose very existence is testimony to the constant cooperation between the social, legal and political and the sacred. One justification for these highly religious State programmes is that the assertive practice of secularism during the early years of the revolution resulted in reduction of the numbers of religious personnel to the extent that the Muslim citizenry began to experience an acute shortage of personnel qualified to officiate important functions like funerals.[186] This impelled the State to intervene to ensure the spiritual lives of its people proceed without hindrance. Active State involvement in religious affairs was also informed by the need to shape the design and delivery of the theological curriculum with the view to fostering a version of Islam that is compatible with the secular philosophy adopted by the Constitution. These 'historical' explanations were given credence by Turkey's Judiciary, which, in response to the Birlik Party's 1971 challenge to the constitutionality of the DRA,[187] confirmed the administrative character of the impugned institution and approved the unique nature of its religious mandate. It was found that certain aspects of religious services were, due to historical conditions, natural and necessary needs of the country.[188]

Similar to Turkey and France, Kenya and Nigeria support certain religious activities. Islamic courts particularly stand out as one area where significant public resources are used to support religious ends in both Kenya and Nigeria. Continued formal existence of these institutions is a consequence of a history that stretches as far back as the 14th century in Kenya and the 9th century in Nigeria. At the East African Coast, Islam suffused the social fabric sufficiently to the extent of being considered the spiritual and cultural way of life.[189] In terms of political administration, a 'caliphate', operated by a Sultan,

---

Turkey." in *Turkey: political, social and economic challenges in the 1990s*, edited by Balim. C *et al*, 1995, p. 95.

186 For a discussion on state intervention in religious affairs in Turkey, Adanali. AH. "The Presidency of Religious Affairs and the Principle of Secularism in Turkey." p. 229.

187 The Birlik Party had contended that the creation of a body of religious personnel goes against both the Ataturk principles and the secular features of the 1961 Constitution. The application also stated that State involvement in religious activities offended the right to freedom of belief and conscience. The irony of a secular state rendering religious services was also questioned.

188 Adanali, AH. "The Presidency of Religious Affairs and the Principle of Secularism in Turkey." p. 235.

189 See, for instance, Martin, BG. "Arab Migrations to East Africa in Medieval Times." p. 367.

governed this system.[190] Disputes among subjects were adjudicated by religious officers (*kadhis*) who drew their wisdom from sharia law.[191] In the area now called Northern Nigeria, communities began to convert to Islam about nine centuries prior to colonialism with the consequence that political establishments founded on sharia were strongly established.[192] The Islamic courts arbitrated over disputes in a wide array of situations including civil and criminal matters.[193]

However, the situation changed drastically when the two countries were put under British control as protectorates on 12 August 1897 and 1 January 1900, respectively, and the common law introduced to the legal systems.[194] On seizing political and juridical authority, colonial authorities permitted religious courts and sharia law to continue having jurisdiction, but only over personal matters.[195]

Despite much debate and resistance in both countries, the compromise to include Islamic courts in the two legal systems survived the independence deliberations of the early 1960s and the constitution-making negotiations that began towards the end of the second millennium. Thus, Nigeria's 1999

190 See, for instance, Martin, BG. "Arab Migrations to East Africa in Medieval Times." p. 367.

191 In this sense, 'sharia' is defined as 'The complete universal code of conduct drawn by the creator, Allah, through His Messenger, Muhammad, detailing the religious, political, economic, social, intellectual and legal systems. It is meant for universal application, covering the entire spectrum of life, prescribing what is lawful (*halal*) and prohibiting what is unlawful (*haram*). Sharia is the Islamic law, which is based on the Quran, the *Hadiths*, and the works of scholars in the first two centuries of Islam.' Ogbu, ON. "Is Nigeria a secular state? Law, Human Rights and Religion in Context." p. 136. In another context it has been written: 'The sharia regulates different aspects of a Muslim's life whether secular or otherwise, such as prayer, dietary regulations, wills and contracts. As a divine law, its authority depends 'on the revealed word of Allah or God.' There are said to be four sources of the sharia: the Koran, *Sunna* (traditions of Prophet Mohammed), *Qiyas* (reasoning by analogy), and *Ijma* (consensus).' Nmehielle, VO. "Sharia Law in The Northern States of Nigeria: To Implement or not to Implement, the Constitutionality is the Question." pp. 732–733.

192 See for instance Yadudu, Auwalu. H. "Colonialism and the Transformation of Islamic Law in the Northern states of Nigeria." *The Journal of Legal Pluralism and Unofficial Law*, vol. 24, no. 32, pp. 103–139.

193 See for instance, Oba. A. A. "Islamic Law as Customary Law: The Changing Perspective in Nigeria." *The International and Comparative Law Quarterly*, vol. 51, no. 4, 2002, pp. 817–850.

194 Bose, Amitabha. "Do All Roads Lead to Islamic Radicalism? A Comparison of Islamic Laws in India and Nigeria." *Georgia Journal of International and Comparative Law*, vol. 32, no. 779, 2004, p. 788.

195 Oba, AA. "Islamic Law as Customary Law: The Changing Perspective in Nigeria." pp. 817–850.

Constitution[196] and Kenya's 2010 Constitution[197] both retain Islamic courts applying sharia to persons professing Islam. However, the two constitutions restrict the application of Islamic courts to matters of personal law. The constitutional provisions on equality in Kenya's Bill of Rights are qualified to the 'extent strictly necessary for the application of Muslim law before the *kadhis*' courts, to persons who profess the Muslim religion, in matters relating to personal status, marriage, divorce and inheritance',[198] while in Nigeria, each state is empowered to establish sharia courts of appeal to determine appeals from lower courts in matters of Islamic personal law.[199]

Notwithstanding the fact that Nigeria's Constitution restrains sharia and *kadhi* courts to personal law matters specifically, Northern states in Nigeria have expanded the jurisdiction of Islamic courts to include criminal proceedings.[200] It was Zamfara that led the way as the first State in Nigeria to fully incorporate sharia,[201] a trend which has been emulated by other northern states and others with large Muslim populations.[202]

Those that advocate for the establishment religious courts dispensing Islamic law usually point out that 'sharia provides a complete code which a true Muslim is bound to respect and practice'.[203] It is also argued that *kadhi* courts 'satisfy the Muslim community's demand for a court that would administer personal laws as Islam requires'.[204] In both countries, opponents have objected to certain aspects of the jurisdiction of religious courts. Sections of the Christian leadership in Kenya litigated against State recognition and funding

196 Article 112, *Constitution of Nigeria* (1999).

197 Article 170, *Constitution of Kenya* (2010).

198 Article 24(4), *Constitution of Kenya* (2010).

199 Bose, A. "Do all Roads Lead to Islamic Radicalism? A Comparison of Islamic Laws in India and Nigeria." *Georgia Journal of International and Comparative Law*, vol. 32, 2004, p. 789. Where established, a sharia court of appeal is headed by a grand *khadi* (or chief judge). It is left to the respective state to prescribe such other *khadis* as may be necessary. See, Bose, A. "Do all Roads Lead to Islamic Radicalism? A Comparison of Islamic Laws in India and Nigeria." p. 790.

200 Rudolph, Peters. "The Re-Islamization of Criminal Law in Northern Nigeria and the Judiciary: The Safiyyatu Hussaini Case." *Sheria, justice and legal Order*, edited by Brill, 2020, pp. 600–601.

201 Bose, A. "Do all Roads Lead to Islamic Radicalism? A Comparison of Islamic Laws in India and Nigeria." p. 791.

202 Bose, A. "Do all Roads Lead to Islamic Radicalism? A Comparison of Islamic Laws in India and Nigeria." p. 791.

203 Ebeku, Kaniye. "Beyond Terrorism: Boko Haram Attacks and National Constitutional Questions in Nigeria." p. 16.

204 Bose, A. "Do all Roads Lead to Islamic Radicalism? A Comparison of Islamic Laws in India and Nigeria." p. 789.

for religious courts arguing that it defeats the very essence of the principle of state-secularism upon which the country is founded.[205] They also made the case against the geographical spread of *kadhi* courts beyond the initial coastal strip.[206] In Nigeria, those in favour of the constitutional project complain about attempts by northern states to expand the jurisdiction of *kadhi* courts to cover criminal law. Already, the comprehensive implementation of sharia in northern states has led to the imposition of sentences more severe than are provided by the Penal Code.[207] For instance, adultery now carries the penalty of death by stoning instead of two years imprisonment, fine, or both under the Penal Code; the penalty for apostasy, which has never been an offence in Nigeria, is also death; in the case of theft or stealing, a limb may be cut from the body.[208]

3.4.1.2 *US Non-Entanglement Policy*

The US 'non-entanglement policy' is diametrically opposed to the model applied in France, Turkey, Kenya and Nigeria in the sense that it erects a high wall between the public purse and the needs of religious institutions. The US policy rests on different considerations altogether. Alive to the oppressive European experience of Christendom that made little distinction between tithes and taxes, church and state, the US designed a secular dispensation whereby public resources are guarded against the endless religious needs.

The US policy position on this aspect was articulated best in the most influential case of *Lemon v Kurtzman*[209] in which the US Supreme Court spoke strongly against the use of public resources in Rhode Island to supplement the salaries of teachers of secular subjects in non-public elementary schools, and Pennsylvania's policy of providing financial support to non-public elementary and secondary schools by way of reimbursement for the cost of teachers' salaries, textbooks, and instructional materials in specified secular subjects. In addition to pointing out the potential of the administration of such programmes degenerating into political contests, the US Supreme Court warned that State surveillance over these mechanisms was likely to lead to unnecessary entanglement with religion, the very mischief the First Amendment sought to

205 See the arguments advanced by *Rev Jesse Kamau in the Jesse Kamau & 25 Others v Attorney General* (2010).

206 *Jesse Kamau and 25 others v Attorney General and Others.* (2010).

207 See, for instance, Nmehielle, VO. "Sharia Law in The Northern States of Nigeria: To Implement or not to Implement, the Constitutionality is the Question." pp. 732–733.

208 Nmehielle, VO. "Sharia Law in The Northern States of Nigeria: To Implement or not to Implement, the Constitutionality is the Question." pp. 732–733.

209 91 Supreme Court 2105 (1971).

ameliorate. While acknowledging that both states had taken some measures to ensure that only teachers of secular subjects in parochial schools would be subsidised, Chief Justice Warren Burger held that it is difficult to ensure teachers in religious schools stick to the secular agenda in the course of their work. Justice Burger recognised that

> [a] dedicated religious person, teaching in a school affiliated with his or her faith and operated to inculcate its tenets, will inevitably experience great difficulty in remaining religiously neutral ... With the best intentions such a teacher would find it hard to make a total separation between secular teaching and religious doctrine.[210]

However, in an earlier decision, *Everson v Board of Education of Ewing TP et al,*[211] the US Supreme Court approved a New Jersey transport reimbursement programme meant for parents with children in both public and religious schools. According to the US Supreme Court, since the programme applied equally to all regardless of religion; and no money was given to religious schools under the scheme, the secular principle of State was not defiled.

3.4.2 State-Secularism and the Politicisation of Religion

In discussing religion and politics, a distinction ought to be made between the politicisation of religious items and the 'religionisation' of politics. The former is part and parcel of normal secular dispensation, as political actors have to take positions on religious issues such as abortion and homosexuality. In the US, the Republican Party champions for value-based issues like school prayers and laws against abortion and homosexuality.[212] While political actors may articulate opinions on religious issues, it is generally problematic for secular states to found politics or political groups on religion. In this connection, Turkey, Kenya, Nigeria and Uganda legislate against the exploitation of religion as the basis for political parties.

Through a combination of various Republican laws, such as the Constitution, the Political Parties' Law, the Law of Associations, and the Criminal Code, Turkey enforces the constitutional requirement that 'sacred religious feelings shall not be involved in state affairs and politics.'[213] Under this framework, it is

---

210 P. 2114.

211 67 Supreme Court 504. Decided 19 February 1947.

212 Pynn, Ronald. E. *American Politics: Changing Expectations*, 4th ed., WCB, Brown & Benchmark Pub, 1993, p. 240.

213 Toprak, B. "Islam and the Secular State in Turkey." See also Preambular paragraph 5, *Turkey's Constitution* (1982).

prohibited to exploit or abuse religion, religious feelings or things held sacred by religion with a view to causing the social, economic, political or legal order of the State to be based on religious precepts, or for the purpose of securing political or personal interest or influence.[214] It is also criminal to take advantage of religion for purposes of propaganda or personal gain.[215] The 1995 elections, which put Prime Minister Necmettin Erbakan's Islamist Welfare Party in power, exemplify this aspect of Turkey's democracy.[216] Due to the fear that the Islamist party would renege on the Kemalist secular philosophy, the military, supported by judicial, political, media, and civil society actors, pressured Erbakan to resign for betraying the secular ideals upon which the State is premised.[217] Similarly, after the 1999 elections, Ms Merve Kavakci was denied the opportunity to take oath as a Member of Parliament while donned in a headscarf (*hijab*).[218] The attempt to take oath while dressed in hijab was interpreted as an anomaly even in the absence of explicit rules of procedure barring hijab in Parliament. According to Kim Shively,

> [t]he very presence of a veiled woman in the Parliament of the secular Turkish Republic provoked a reaction so intense and pervasive that the Turkish government erupted in condemnation, citizens took to the streets in protest, and the woman herself ended up barred from her job and stripped of her citizenship.[219]

Similar to Turkey, Kenya, Nigeria and Uganda forbid the founding of political parties on religious basis.[220] They also bar political parties from using words, slogans, emblems or symbols with the potential of arousing religious divisions. Nigeria's electoral laws go as far as proscribing political campaigns based on religion.[221]

214 Article 24, *Turkey's Constitution* (1982).

215 Kuru, AT. *Secularism and State Policies toward Religion*. p. 162.

216 Kuru, AT. *Secularism and State Policies toward Religion*. p. 162.

217 Kuru, AT. *Secularism and State Policies toward Religion*. p. 162.

218 Shively, K. "Religious Bodies and the Secular State: The Merve Kavakci Affair." Journal of Middle East Women's Studies, vol. 1, 2005, p. 46.

219 Shively, K. "Religious Bodies and the Secular State: The Merve Kavakci Affair." p. 46.

220 Article 91(2), Constitution of Kenya (2010); Section 222, Constitution of the Federal Republic of Nigeria (1999); Article 71, Constitution of the Republic of Uganda (1995).

221 Section 102, Electoral Act, Nigeria.

Part 4: The Right to Freedom of Religion: Case Study of the Treatment of Religion in Educational Institutions

The discussion in Part 3 reveals the diversity of the practice of state-secularism and the difficulty in identifying any common thread. Building on that discussion, I demonstrate that despite ratifying the major international human rights instruments,[222] and the constitutionalising of their provisions on the right to freedom of religion, including the freedom to manifest religious belief, emerging judicial jurisprudence in Kenya and Uganda is against open manifestation of religion through religious attire (in Kenya) and through the observance of the Sabbath (in Kenya and Uganda). I argue further that notwithstanding the finding above that there is no standard practice of state-secularism, this restrictive approach is based on a common but warped understanding of the concept of state secularism, which equates it to animosity toward external manifestation of religion. In this regard, the reforms in France since 2004 (eliminating religious manifestation from the public sphere) and Turkey (during the material time) could have influenced Kenya's initial judicial jurisprudence on religious attire; while the changes in Turkey in the last decade (reconsidering the erstwhile tough secular stance on religious dressing) may have contributed to the attempts to review the judicial policy in the country. With regards to religious instruction, all the African study countries continue the colonial legacy of using the westernised educational platforms as forums for evangelism[223] sometimes without providing alternatives to accommodate the wishes of parents and guardians for children that belong to other religions or to no religion at all, contrary to international human rights law.[224]

I focus on the right to freedom of religion because there is a direct correlation between it and the concept of state-secularism. Indeed, it is a truism that secular states guarantee the right to freedom of religion and a country's secularism depends on the 'amount' of religious freedom its people enjoy.[225]

222 Kenya acceded to the International Covenant on Civil and Political Rights on 1 May 1972, while Uganda did so on 21 June 1995. https://treaties.un.org/pages/ViewDetails.aspx?src=TREATY&mtdsg_no=IV-4&chapter=4&clang=_en. Accessed on 18 September 2020.

223 Albeit with some modifications.

224 *CCPR General Comment* 22, 1994, UN Doc HRI/GEN/1/Rev at pp. 35, 6.

225 This is the reason why, even in the absence of express recognition of the principle of state-secularism or neutrality in the European Convention on Human Rights, the European Court on Human Rights' jurisprudence acknowledges its usefulness in the realisation of the right to freedom of religion. See, for instance, Martinez-Torron, Javier. "Freedom of Religion in the European Convention on Human Rights under the Influence of Different European traditions." www.pass.va/content/dam Accessed on 16 April 2015. According to

I highlight educational institutions because they have proven to be the main battlefronts in the contest between those who seek a bigger role for religion in the public sphere and those in favour of strict limitations to the freedom to manifest religion.[226]

International human rights law has evolved principles that constitute the right to freedom of religion. Using this normative framework, I now track the practice of the right to freedom of religion in educational institutions in the study countries.

4.1 *The Normative Framework: The Right to Freedom of Religion in International Human Rights Law*

To the extent that the right to freedom of thought, conscience and religion is carried in all major human rights instruments,[227] it is an entrenched member of the human rights family. This freedom has 'internal' and 'external' components.[228] The internal constituent of the right is 'psychological' or 'mental' in the sense that it is 'primarily a matter of individual conscience'.[229] It entails the freedom of thought or belief in certain religious doctrines. The external element is about the freedom to manifest one's religion.[230] A believer may manifest their religion by engaging in an inexhaustible list of observable religious phenomena, which include the following freedoms:

> To worship or assemble in connection with a religion or belief, and to establish and maintain places for these purposes;

the Human Rights Committee: 'The fact that a religion is recognised as a state religion or that it is established as official or traditional or that its followers comprise the majority of the population, shall not result in any impairment of the enjoyment of any of the rights under the Covenant, including articles 18 and 27, nor in any discrimination against adherents to other religions or non-believers.' *CCPR General Comment* 22, 1994, UN Doc HRI/GEN/1/Rev at p. 35, 9.

226 Ahmet Kuru observed that historical and contemporary debates on secularism in France, Turkey and the US 'have pointed to education as the main battlefield in state-religion controversies'. See, Kuru, AT. "Passive and assertive secularism: historical Conditions, Ideological Struggles, and State Polices toward Religion." p. 569.

227 See, for instance, article 18, UDHR; article 18, CCPR; and article 8, African Charter.

228 Attiya Waris, however, breaks the right to freedom of religion into first, the extent to which a particular religion may be recognised by a state and secondly the freedom to exercise it, see, Waris, Attiya. "Making a mountain out of a molehill: The protection of the right to the freedom of religion of the Muslim religious minority in Kenya's Constitution." *International Journal on Minority and Group Rights* vol. 14, 2007, p. 25.

229 *Leyla Sahin v Turkey*, ECtHR Judgement of 10 November 2005, para. 105.

230 *Leyla Sahin v Turkey*, ECtHR, para. 105.

> To establish and maintain appropriate charitable or humanitarian institutions;
>
> To make, acquire and use to an adequate extent the necessary articles and materials related to the rites or customs of a religion or belief;
>
> To write, issue and disseminate relevant publications in these areas;
>
> To teach a religion or belief in places suitable for these purposes;
>
> To solicit and receive voluntary financial and other contributions from individuals and institutions;
>
> To train, appoint, elect or designate by succession appropriate leaders called for by the requirements and standards of any religion or belief;
>
> To observe days of rest and to celebrate holidays and ceremonies in accordance with the precepts of one's religion or belief; and
>
> To establish and maintain communications with individuals and communities in matters of religion and belief at the national and international levels.[231]

This broad terrain of observable religious phenomena situates the right to freedom of religion within an interlocking web consisting nine or so other general liberties, namely: freedom of communication and expression; freedom of association; freedom of peaceful assembly; freedom of political participation; freedom of movement; economic liberties; privacy and autonomy in the areas of home, family, sexuality and reproduction; and freedom to follow an ethic, plan of life, lifestyle, or traditional way of living.[232]

The right to freedom of religion liberates individuals from coercion which would impair their freedom to adopt a religion of their own choice.[233] This principle was affirmed in the case of *Free Legal Assistance Group and Others v Zaire*[234] where the African Commission on Human and Peoples' Rights (the African Commission) declared the harassment and arbitrary arrests of members of a religious sect, Jehovah Witness, a violation of Article 8 of the African Charter on Human and Peoples' Rights (African Charter). The African Commission has also spoken against sharia courts' jurisdiction over non-Muslims in Sudan, finding that 'it is fundamentally unjust that religious laws

---

231 Article 6, UNGA, *Declaration on the Elimination of All Forms of Intolerance and of Discrimination Based on Religion or Belief*, UN A/RES/36/55 25 November 1981.

232 Nickel, JW. "Who Needs Freedom of Religion?" *University of Colorado Law Review*, vol. 76, 2005, p. 943.

233 Article 18(2), International Covenant on Civil and Political Rights of 1976.

234 *Free Legal Assistance Group and Others v Zaire*, ACmHPR Comm. No. 25/89, 47/90, 56/91, 100/93 (1995).

should be applied against non-adherents of the religion'.[235] In view of these scenarios, the right to freedom of religion excludes 'any discretion on the part of the state to determine whether religious beliefs or the means used to express such beliefs are legitimate'.[236]

While adults are entitled to adopt a religion of their own choice, it is incumbent upon parents or legal guardians to identify for their children the religious and moral education which they consider appropriate.[237] Reigning international human rights law principles recognise the liberty of parents or legal guardians 'to organise the life within the family in accordance with their religion or belief, bearing in mind the moral education in which they believe the child should be brought up.'[238] In the case of children not under the due care of any parent or guardian, it is advised that their views on religion or belief be taken into consideration, the best interests' principle being the guiding philosophy.[239] Consistent with this overarching framework is the requirement that children be brought up in a manner that is not injurious to their physical or mental health or their full development.[240]

In public schools and other institutions of learning, the right to freedom of religion means refraining from instruction of a particular religion of belief, 'unless provision is made for non-discriminatory exemptions or alternatives that would accommodate the wishes of parents and guardians'.[241] However, education in subjects like the general history of religions and ethics may be offered to all students in public schools so long as it is delivered in a neutral and objective manner.[242]

Like other human rights, the right to freedom of thought, conscience and religion is subject to limitations meant to protect public safety, order, health, or morals or the fundamental rights and freedoms of others.[243] It is also generally understood that the protection of the right to freedom of religion does not

---

235 *Amnesty International and Others v Sudan*, ACmHPR Comm. 48/90, 50/91, 89/93 (1999), para. 73.

236 Case of *Manoussakis and Others v Greece*, ECtHR Judgment of 26 September 1996, para. 47.

237 Article 18(4), International Covenant on Civil and Political Rights of 1976.

238 Article 5(1), UNGA, *Declaration on the Elimination of All Forms of Intolerance and of Discrimination Based on Religion or Belief.*

239 Article 5(4), UNGA, *Declaration on the Elimination of All Forms of Intolerance and of Discrimination Based on Religion or Belief.*

240 Article 5(5), UNGA, *Declaration on the Elimination of All Forms of Intolerance and of Discrimination Based on Religion or Belief.*

241 *CCPR, General Comment* 22, 35.

242 *CCPR, General Comment* 22, 6.

243 See, article 18(3), *International Covenant on Civil and Political Rights.*

cover any practices which 'may amount to propaganda for war or advocacy of national, racial or religious hatred that constitutes incitement to discrimination, hostility or violence'.[244] However, since the 'internal' component of the right to freedom of religion operates within the realm of the conscience and therefore has no immediate implications on public safety, order, health, or the rights of others, it is arguably absolute. This is because the human conscience is inviolable. A final point to note is that the right to freedom of religion is not restricted in its application to traditional religions or to religions and beliefs with institutional characteristics.[245]

4.2 *The Right to Freedom of Religion in the Study Countries*

All the study countries articulate the right to freedom of religion either through the constitution or other important legislations or instruments. The French Declaration of the Rights of Man and the Citizen (1789) long established that 'no one should be disturbed for his opinions, even in religion, provided that their manifestation does not trouble public order as established by law'.[246] In 1905, this right was extended through the enactment of penal sanctions providing

> [f]or the punishment of those who utilise violent acts or threats against an individual (creating either fear of job loss or causing injury to the individual's person, family, or wealth) to force that individual to participate, or to refrain from participating, in a religion.[247]

Article 24 of Turkey's Constitution guarantees everyone the right to freedom of conscience, belief and religion and the free exercise of religious activities like prayers, worship and religious services. The provision also forbids censorship or persecution of individuals and groups on the basis of their religious beliefs or convictions. Apart from compulsory instruction in religious culture and morals as part of the curricula of primary and secondary schools through which the State ensures that pupils/students are first exposed to 'acceptable'

244 *CCPR, General Comment* 22, 7.

245 *CCPR, General Comment* 22, 2.

246 Article 10 of the Declaration. The Declaration was approved by the National Assembly of France on 26 August 1789.

247 See Robert, Jacques. "Religious liberty and French secularism." *Brigham Young University Law Review*, 2003, p. 644; quoting article 31 of the Law of 1905; quoting article 31 of the Law of 1905.

interpretation of Islam before learning other religious teachings,[248] Turkey's Constitution directs that other religious education and instruction shall be a matter for individual choice, with the decision in the case of minors being taken by their legal guardians.[249] In sync with the international normative framework discussed above, all human rights in Turkey are subject to limitations. More specifically, the enjoyment of the right to freedom of religion should not threaten the indivisible integrity of the State with its territory and nation, and the existence of the democratic and secular order of the Republic based on human rights.[250]

The US, like France and Turkey, is faithful to the secular tradition of protecting the right to freedom of conscience, thought and faith for its Constitution recognises the liberty of everyone to profess a belief or disbelief in any religion.[251] This entitlement has been given great impetus by the jurisprudence of the US Supreme Court. In *Wallace v Jaffree*,[252] Justice John Paul Stevens was categorical that

> [t]he First Amendment was adopted to curtail the power of Congress to interfere with the individual's freedom to believe, to worship, and to express himself in accordance with the dictates of his own conscience.[253]

In the case of *State of Wisconsin v Jonas Yoder*,[254] the US Supreme Court upheld the wish of Amish parents to exempt their children (who had studied up to grade eight) from a Wisconsin State policy, which made it mandatory for all children to attend school till grade twelve. The US Supreme Court agreed with the Amish parents that their religion, which teaches simple non-competitive Christian life un-obsessed with material success, should be shielded from the domineering values taught by modern educational systems. The US highest judicial tribunal exalted the place of religious freedom in relation to other

248 All students/pupils in Turkey are exposed to State designed religious (Islamic) curriculum. Gunn, TJ. "French Secularism as Utopia and Myth." *Houston Law Review*, vol. 42, 2006, p. 82.

249 The Turkish State, however, reserves for itself the task of supervising and controlling education and instruction in religion and ethics.

250 Article 14, Turkish Constitution.

251 See, the First Amendment.

252 *Wallace v Jaffree* (1985) The Supreme Court of the United States.

253 *Wallace v Jaffree* (1985).

254 *State of Wisconsin v Jonas Yoder* (1972) The Supreme Court of the United States.

competing interests like education and recognised the place of parental direction in the religious upbringing and education of their children.[255]

Kenya's resolve to assert a secular constitutional order through religious freedom starts at the very beginning; in its preamble. Here, the people announce their pride 'in the ethnic, cultural and religious diversity of the nation'.[256] But it is in the Bill of Rights that the State's equal treatment policy towards religion is effectively conveyed. In the first instance, there is a promise to treat everyone equally and to bar discrimination on an elaborate list of grounds, including religion and conscience.[257] Ultimately, Kenya's Constitution guarantees that:

> (1) Every person has the right to freedom of conscience, religion, thought, belief and opinion.
> (2) Every person has the right, either individually or in community with others, in public or in private, to manifest any religion or belief through worship, practice, teaching or observance, including observance of a day of worship.
> (3) A person may not be denied access to any institution, employment or facility, or the enjoyment of any right, because of the person's belief or religion.
> (4) A person shall not be compelled to act, or engage in any act, that is contrary to the person's belief or religion.[258]

The exercise of these rights is subject to limitations that are

> [r]easonable and justifiable in an open and democratic society based on human dignity, equality and freedom, taking into account all relevant factors, including – the nature of the right or fundamental freedom; the importance of the purpose of the limitation; the nature and extent of the limitation; the need to ensure that the enjoyment of rights and fundamental freedoms by any individual does not prejudice the rights and

255 Chief Justice Burger held: 'Long before there was general acknowledgement of the need for universal formal education, the Religion Clauses had specifically and firmly fixed the right to free exercise of religious beliefs, and buttressing this fundamental right was an equally firm, even if less explicit, prohibition against the establishment of any religion by government. The values underlying these two provisions relating to religion have been zealously protected, sometimes even at the expense of other interests of admittedly high social importance.'

256 Preambular para. 8.

257 Article 27(4), *Constitution of Kenya* (2010).

258 Article 32, *Constitution of Kenya* (2010).

> fundamental freedoms of others; and the relation between the limitation and its purpose and whether there are less restrictive means to achieve the purpose …[259]

As with all the above study countries, the right to freedom of religion in Nigeria's Constitution is modelled along international human rights law principles. To begin with, Nigeria's Bill of Rights prohibits discrimination on an elaborate list of categories,[260] including specifically the ground of religion.[261] There is also express constitutional guarantee of the right to freedom of thought, conscience and religion.[262] In exercise of this right, a person may change religion or belief, and may freely manifest and propagate such faith through worship, teaching, practice and observance.[263] Nigeria's Constitution additionally protects persons in educational institutions from forceful religious instruction, practices and ceremonies of denominations to which they do not belong.[264] At the same time, religious denominations that own or run educational institutions are entitled, at their facilities, to offer religious instruction to students or pupils that are followers of their faith.[265]

The enjoyment of the right to freedom of religion in Nigeria is subject to internal and external of limitations.[266] The internal limitation, which is carried in the very article that articulates the religious liberty, provides that the right to freedom of religion does not entitle one to belong or take part in activities

259 Article 24, *Constitution of Kenya* (2010).

260 The other grounds include: place of origin, sex, status, ethnic or linguistic association or ties.

261 Section 15(2), *1999 Constitution of Nigeria*; section 42(1) 1999 *Constitution of Nigeria.*

262 Section 38(1), *1999 Constitution of Nigeria.*

263 Section 38(1), *1999 Constitution of Nigeria.*

264 Section 38(2), *1999 Constitution of Nigeria.*

265 Section 38(3), *1999 Constitution of Nigeria*. Since the colonial times: "The different Christian missions used school as an organ of religious instruction, character formation, skill acquisition and initiation into the three basic elements of reading, writing and arithmetic. Among other crucial roles of the missionary enterprise were the establishment of mission hospitals and leprosy settlements; agriculture and farm settlements and providing worthwhile training and jobs for Africans in Nigeria. The missionary team included white missionaries, a medical man, an ordained educationalist and a horticulturalist (African Missions 2010:15). Some have commented that the rapid expansion of education, particularly in southern Nigeria, was actually the accidental outcome of missionary rivalry between Catholic and Protestant Missionaries rather than the result of an altruistic policy to provide expanded educational opportunities for the Nigerian populace (Bassey 1997:47)." See – Miracle, Ajah. "Religious education and nation-building in Nigeria." *Stellenbosch Theological Journal*, Vol 1, No 2, 2015, pp. 263–282, pp. 267–269.

266 See, Nwauche, Enyinna. S. "Law, Religion and Human Rights in Nigeria." p. 36.

of secret societies.[267] In this regard, in *Henry O Awoniyi & ORS v The Registered Trustees of the Rosicrucian Order, AMORC (NIG)*,[268] the Supreme Court of Nigeria determined that an organisation whose aim is stated as being to vitalise and prolong human life, whose documents openly describe it as secret, and which engages in occult teachings, qualifies to be called a secret society; and is therefore unlawful. The external limitation clause replicates that found in the CCPR; it states:

> Nothing in sections 37, 38, 39, 40 and 41 of this Constitution shall invalidate any law that is reasonably justifiable in a democratic society (a) in the interest of defence, public safety, public order, public morality or public health; or (b) for the purpose of protecting the rights and freedom of other persons.[269]

In Uganda, there is a commitment 'to promote a culture of cooperation, understanding, appreciation, tolerance and respect for each other's customs, traditions and beliefs'[270] and to eliminate discrimination on the ground of religion, among others.[271] Additionally, Uganda protects the freedom of thought, conscience and belief[272] as well as the

> [f]reedom to practice any religion and manifest such practice which shall include the right to belong to and participate in the practices of

267 Section 38(4), *1999 Nigerian Constitution.* By 'secret society' is meant 'any society, association, group or body of persons (whether registered or not) (a) that uses secret signs, oaths, rites or symbols and which is formed to promote a cause, the purpose or part of the purpose of which is to foster the interest of its members and to aid one another under any circumstances without due regard to merit, fair play or justice to the detriment of the legitimate interest of those who are not members; (b) the membership of which is incompatible with the function or dignity of any public office under this Constitution and whose members are sworn to observe oaths of secrecy; or (c) the activities of which are not known to the public at large, the names of whose members are kept secret and whose meetings and other activities are held in secret.' See – Section 318, *1999 Nigerian Constitution.*

268 *Henry O Awoniyi & ORS v The Registered Trustees of the Rosicrucian Order, AMORC (NIG)*, available at https://lawcarenigeria.com/henry-o-awoniyi-ors-v-the-reg-trustees-of-the-rosicrucian-order-amorc-nig. Accessed 30 September 2020.

269 Article 45(1), 1999 Nigerian Constitution.

270 Constitution of the Republic of Uganda, 1995. Part III of the National Objectives and Directive Principles of State Policy on 'national unity and stability'.

271 Article 21(3), Constitution of Uganda, 1995.

272 Article 29(1)(b), Constitution of Uganda, 1995.

> any religious body or organisation in a manner consistent with the constitution.[273]

Further, every person in Uganda has the right to 'enjoy, practice, profess, maintain and promote any culture, cultural institution, language, tradition, creed, or religion in community with others'.[274]

In line with the international principles, the enjoyment of religious freedom in Uganda applies only to the extent that such liberty does not prejudice the fundamental human rights and freedoms of others or the public interest.[275] In this connection, the Constitutional Court of Uganda has made a distinction between the freedom of thought or conscience, which involves holding to one's beliefs freely, and the freedom to manifest one's religion or belief. The former is absolute in the sense that it cannot be subjected to coercion or compulsion. The latter 'is subject to such limitations that are necessary in the public interest, which limitations have to be prescribed by law and are necessary in a democratic society'.[276]

With near unanimity, all the study countries incorporate the right to freedom of religion in their constitutions. It is a sign that the right to freedom of religion is a critical component for secular dispensations, and also that there is general consensus on its meaning.

4.3 *Religious Instruction in Comparative Perspective*

With the exception of the US and to a limited extent France, all the other study countries support some form of religious instruction using public resources. Much as religious instruction in Turkey and France is for secular ends; for the African study countries, religious instruction is a continuation of the missionary and colonial legacy which is mainly to the detriment of African religion. This preferential system continues to thrive even with the normative international and municipal framework on the right to freedom of religion discussed above.

Turkey offers compulsory instruction in religious culture and morals in primary and secondary schools[277] to provide doctrinal support for the ideals of

273 Article 29(1)(c), Constitution of Uganda, 1995.

274 Article 37, Constitution of Uganda, 1995.

275 Article 43(1), Constitution of Uganda, 1995.

276 Constitutional Court of Uganda Petition No 15 of 2006 – involving Caroline Turyatemba, Allan Elwana Okiror, Ogwang Richard, Ephraim Byamukama and Barham Banyenzaki against the Attorney General and the Uganda Land Commission.

277 All students/pupils in Turkey are exposed to State designed religious (Islamic) curriculum. Gunn, TJ. "French Secularism as Utopia and Myth." p. 90.

the Kemal Atatürk revolution[278] and to minimise chances of fundamentalist Islam radicalising young learners.[279] Controlled religious instruction was considered desirable in the post-revolution era not only because the Kemalist's had overthrown a caliphate, the Ottoman Empire, but also they insisted on a secular democratic order – a very rare development in the Middle East.[280] Sustaining the quite radical secular democratic order required appropriate theology, which the State undertook to offer in the form of compulsory religious instruction.[281] Today, controlled religious instruction in schools can also be seen as a response to fundamentalist Islam, which many commentators blame for the escalating cases of terrorism in the region and beyond.[282] Thus, compulsory religious instruction in Turkey aims at exposing learners to 'acceptable' interpretation of Islam both to sustain the secular and democratic ideals of the State and to neutralise Islamic radicalism.[283]

As a general principle France does not oblige religious instruction in educational institutions. However, there are limited exceptions to this rule. Religious communities in France are availed the latitude to operate chaplaincies meant to offer religious counselling and instruction to students within school compounds.[284] In public schools where chaplaincies are not established, school schedules are normally changed in order to allow learners to receive religious instruction outside public schools.[285] In fact, it is a legal requirement for schools to close one additional day every week to give parents a chance to present their children to catechism classes of choice.[286] In addition, Alsace and Moselle are exempted from the general rule proscribing religious instruction[287] because the regions were under the control of Germany at

278 Danforth, Nicholas. "Ideology and Pragmatism in Turkish foreign policy: From Atatürk to the AKP." *Turkish Policy Quarterly*, 2008, p. 88.

279 Brown, James. "Islamic Fundamentalism and Turkey." *Journal of Political and Military Sociology*, vol. 16, no. 2, 1988, pp. 235–246.

280 Kuru, AT. "Passive and Assertive Secularism", pp. 14, 27, and 163–164.

281 Danforth, Nicholas. "Ideology and Pragmatism in Turkish Foreign Policy: From Atatürk to the AKP," p. 88.

282 See, Minkiewicz, Margot Stańczyk. "Interdependencies between religion, fundamentalism and terrorism." *European Journal of Science and Theology*, vol. 16, no. 4, 2020, pp. 101–113.

283 All students/pupils in Turkey are exposed to State designed religious (Islamic) curriculum. Gunn, TJ. "French Secularism as Utopia and Myth." p. 90.

284 Gunn, TJ. "French Secularism as Utopia and Myth." p. 90.

285 Troper, M. "French Secularism, or Laicité." p. 1277.

286 Troper, M. "French Secularism, or Laicité." p. 1277.

287 Gunn, TJ. "French Secularism as Utopia and Myth." p. 90.

the point the secular order was established.[288] Recently, France introduced the 'secular teaching of religious facts' ostensibly in reaction to religious radicalism believed to be responsible for a number of terror attacks in the country.[289]

The US disentangles itself from religion by maintaining a safe distance between public educational institutions and faith-based activities including religious instruction. In *People of State of Illinois ex rel. McCollum v Board of Education of School District No 71, Champaign County, Illinois et al*,[290] the US Supreme Court declared a programme whereby a consortium of religious groups would organise weekly doctrinal classes for pupils whose parents consented to the scheme unconstitutional. The US Supreme Court ruled against the use of buildings belonging to public schools for religious instruction and the invaluable aid given to religious sects to inculcate their beliefs. The US Supreme Court concluded that the influence exerted upon children by their institutions of learning to attend religious classes was offensive to the First Amendment.[291] According to Justice Felix Frankfurter, 'in no activity of the State is it more vital to keep out divisive forces than in its schools, to avoid confusing, not to say fusing, what the Constitution sought to keep strictly apart.'[292] In another decision, *Wallace v Jaffree*, the US Supreme Court found an Alabama statute, which sought to introduce voluntary prayer in addition to meditation in schools as falling below the constitutional muster. In *Lemon v Kurtzman* the US Supreme Court disapproved the use of public resources to fund salaries of teachers of secular subjects, textbooks, and instructional materials in specified secular subjects in non-public elementary schools arguing mainly that this was likely to lead to unnecessary entanglement with religion. However, US Supreme Court certified a transport reimbursement programme for parents with children in both public and religious schools that applied equally to all regardless of religion and did not transfer monies to religious schools.[293] These precedents illustrate that the US secular policy stands for separation between public schools and religious activities such as prayer and instruction.

288 Carrola, Alison and Zanoun, Louisa. "The view from the border: a comparative study of autonomism in Alsace and the Moselle, 1918–29." *European Review of History – Revue europe'enne d'histoire*, vol. 18, no. 4, 2011, p. 476.

289 See, "The Fine Line of Teaching Religion in France's Secular Schools." *The Local.* https://www.thelocal.fr/20171020/the-fine-line-of-teaching-religion-in-frances-secular-schools. Accessed on 18 September 2020.

290 68 Supreme Court 461.

291 Page 466. As per Black J.

292 Page 475. As per Frankfurter J.

293 *Everson v Board of Education of Ewing TP et al.*

Religious instruction is part of the national school curriculums of Kenya, Nigeria and Uganda. The African study countries are similar in three important respects. First, in all of them, religious instruction as a feature of formal educational institutions was started by missionaries prior to colonialism.[294] British colonial regimes accommodated and even encouraged particularly the Christian missionary influence in education. Second, despite post-independence secular and developmental educational policies, the respective curriculums continue to accommodate instruction in Christian, Hindu and Islamic religions – at their best. At their worst, the systems favour only either Abrahamic religion. Finally, in all cases there is limited room for African religion.

4.3.1 The Missionary and Colonial Roots

Christianity as a predominant missionary religion was first introduced to Kenya by Portuguese explorers and traders in the early 16th century.[295] However, the Portuguese were unsuccessful in founding notable educational institutions despite inhabiting the Kenyan coast for nearly three centuries.[296] It was not until the 1840s – with the arrival of Ludwig Krapf and Johann Rebmann both of the Church Missionary Society (CMS) – that proper foundation for missionary education was laid.[297] The initial motivation of the Christian missionaries was to evangelise the native Africans.[298] But the missionaries soon realised that evangelism would be impossible without basic literacy in western methods and a general appreciation of its civilisation. This necessitated the establishment of formal schools,[299] which still characterise Christian missionary work in Kenya today.

When colonialism commenced in earnest after the 1890s, Christian missionary education complemented the British imperial policy "to correct and

---

294 Lekwat, Barnaba B. "*The development of religious education in Nigeria.*" Barnaba Bariyakaad Lekwat, 1984.

295 Chandra Richard, De Silva. "Indian Ocean but not African Sea." *Journal of Black Studies*, vol. 29, no. 5, 1999, pp. 684–694.

296 Itolondo, Wilfrida. "The role and status of Christian Religious Education in the school curriculum in Kenya." *Journal of Emerging Trends in Educational Research and Policy Studies*, vol. 3, 2012, p. 721.

297 Itolondo, Wilfrida. "The role and status of Christian Religious Education in the school curriculum in Kenya." p. 721.

298 Itolondo, Wilfrida. "The role and status of Christian Religious Education in the school curriculum in Kenya." p. 721.

299 Itolondo, Wilfrida. "The role and status of Christian Religious Education in the school curriculum in Kenya." p. 721.

Christianise the 'native' customs of the colonies under their control".[300] This explains why the colonial administration supported Christian missionaries through granting them the freedom to start and operate schools on their own terms, and providing financial aid to the schools, among other measures.[301]

Although Islamic schools were also established during the colonial epoch, their numbers and influence was considerably lesser. Since the arrival of Islam at the East African coast in the 9th century, Islamic instruction was delivered through informal Islamic schools (Madrasas) and Qur'anic schools. Attempts to establish formal Islamic schools during the colonial epoch were not as successful as their Christian equivalents mainly because the British colonial officials did not support them.[302] Post-independence reforms introduced IRE as a formal subject in primary and secondary schools but the course has suffered a shortage of teachers throughout the country.[303] To compensate for this shortfall many Muslim learners in secular schools attend Madrassa and Qur'anic schools to seek Islamic education in the evening and on weekends.[304] Additionally, the fears that children might 'lose their identity as Muslims due to the strong non-Islamic influence in the formal schools' has led to the recent trends to establish Islamic integrated schools particularly in regions with large settlements of Muslims. The integrated schools amalgamate the Qur'anic

300 Hepple, J. "Will Sexual Minorities ever be Equal? The Repercussions of British Colonial "Sodomy" laws." The Equal Rights Review, vol. 8, 2012, p. 54. See, also Isaack, Mohamed Aloi. "Islamic Education in Kenya from Colonial Period to Date." *International Academic Journal of Social Sciences and Education* (*IAJSSE*), 2018, pp. 5–6, where it is stated: "The mission's educational objective was not only to expose Africans to a superior culture, but also to instruct pupils in the Word of God. Missionaries wanted Christian "truths" spread into the villages and countryside. The missionaries, dedicated to indoctrinating the African with a Christian moral code and knowledge that could be applied to the "betterment" of the tribal community, insisted it was necessary to coordinate education with religion. Missionaries saw in education a means by which to extend Christianity."

301 See, Isaack, Mohamed Aloi. "Islamic Education in Kenya from Colonial Period to Date." pp. 5–6.

302 See, Isaack, Mohamed Aloi. "Islamic Education in Kenya from Colonial Period to Date." p. 5. where it is stated: "The missionary societies pressed the colonial administration to be allowed to take charge of African education with a view to building a Christian foundation. This view was supported by the various education commissions that were set up before Kenya's independence."

303 See Isaack, Mohamed Aloi. "Islamic Education in Kenya from Colonial Period to Date." p. 8.

304 Abdi, Adel Ali. "Integration of Islamic and Secular Education in Kenya: A synthesis of the Literature" *International Journal of Social Science and Humanities Research*, vol. 5, no. 3, 2017, p. 67.

schools, traditional Madrasa institutions and secular formal schooling.[305] Integrated schools are meeting the "demand for Islamic education to satisfy religious needs and demand for secular education to get socialized to the labour market and understand the secular world."[306]

The dominance of Christian education in Nigeria (particularly Southern Nigeria) is usually traced to the arrival (in Badagry, Southwest Nigeria) of Thomas Freeman of the Wesleyan Methodist Movement and Henry Townsend of the Church Missionary Society of the Church of England in 1842[307] – just about the same time Krapf and Rebmann reported in Kenya. Until 1925, when the education policy was reviewed to accord other school subjects equality with religious and moral instruction, Christian religious instruction was the foundation subject of the Nigerian colonial educational system.[308] According to Ajah Miracle '[t]he different Christian missions used school as an organ of religious instruction, character formation, skill acquisition and initiation into the three basic elements of reading, writing and arithmetic'.[309] Up to independence in 1960, children attending Christian mission schools had to study confessional Christian Religious Knowledge and attend compulsory school assemblies which took place at the beginning of each day regardless of their religious beliefs.[310] A century after the arrival of the pioneer Christian educationists (in 1942), it was estimated that the missions controlled 99% of Nigeria's schools and 97% of all students were in missionary schools.[311] But this rapid expansion should not always be mistaken for passionate pursuit for African education. It is arguable that expansion of education institutions, especially in southern Nigeria, was a result of rivalry between Catholic and Protestant

305 See, Isaack, Mohamed Aloi. "Islamic Education in Kenya from Colonial Period to Date." p. 4.

306 Aden, Ali. Abdi. "Integration of Islamic and secular education in Kenya: A synthesis of the literature", *International Journal of Social Science and Humanities Research* vol. 5, no. 3, 2017, p. 67.

307 Jawaniyi, Oduntan. "Rethinking the Religious Education Curricula in Nigerian Schools." *Journal for the Study of Religion* vol. 22, no. 2, 2009, p. 65.

308 Lekwat, Barnaba. B. "The development of religious education in Nigeria."

309 Ajah Miracle. "Religious education and nation-building in Nigeria." pp. 267–269.

310 Jawaniyi, Oduntan. "Rethinking the Religious Education Curricula in Nigerian Schools." pp. 86 and 66.

311 Jawaniyi, Oduntan. "Rethinking the Religious Education Curricula in Nigerian Schools." p. 68.

missionaries rather than the result of an altruistic policy to provide expanded educational opportunities for native Nigerians.[312]

Although Christian missionary education has been dominant in Nigeria, informal Islamic schools based on the Quran and related teachings were the first foreign educational system to be established.[313] Islam arrived in Northern Nigeria through trade routes in the 9th century and by the time the British Empire declared the Nigerian colony in 1914, Islamic schools had been so entrenched that not even colonial educational interventions in the region succeeded easily.[314] Like their Christian counterparts, Islamic schools during the colonial epoch insisted on compulsory Islamic Religious Knowledge and school assemblies.[315]

In the same way as in Kenya and Nigeria, it is Christian missionaries that introduced religious instruction and even formal schools in Uganda during the colonial epoch. From 1925 the colonial government began to conduct education through building and administering some schools.[316] However, this did not diminish the missions, which continued to invest significant resources to advance their educational programmes.[317] Similar to Kenya and Nigeria, Islamic schools were also established during and after the colonial epoch, although they were vastly outnumbered.[318] The few Muslims (mostly traders) that inhabited Uganda initially made no attempts at starting an education system until the 1930s when the dilemma of having to attend Christian schools impelled such initiatives.[319]

312 Jawaniyi, Oduntan. "Rethinking the Religious Education Curricula in Nigerian Schools." pp. 267–269.

313 Baba, Mohammed. Nasir. "Islamic Schools, the Ulama, and the State in the Educational Development of Northern Nigeria." *LIT Verlag*, vol. 33, 2011, pp. 1–2.

314 Baba, Mohammed. Nasir. "Islamic Schools, the Ulama, and the State in the Educational Development of Northern Nigeria." pp. 1–2.

315 Jawaniyi, Oduntan. "Rethinking the Religious Education Curricula in Nigerian Schools." pp. 63–86, 67.

316 See Lewis, Joanna. *Empire State-building: War & Welfare in Kenya, 1925–52*. Ohio University Press, 2000.

317 For a detailed discussion of educational development in Uganda, see Ssekamwa. J.G. *History and Development of Education in Uganda*, Fountain Publishers, 1997.

318 Nimrod, Muhumuza. *The Constitutionality of Religious Education in Uganda*. Global Campus Africa, 2018, p. 26.

319 Reuben, Musiime. "A Critical Evaluation of The Religious Education Curriculum for Secondary School Students In Uganda", dissertation presented to the Graduate Council of the University of North Texas in partial fulfillment of the requirements for the degree of Doctor of Philosophy, December 1996. p. 28.

4.3.2 Post-Independence Policies

A year into independence (in 1964), Kenya's founding President Jomo Kenyatta established a Commission of Inquiry to survey the existing educational resources and to advise the Government in the formulation and implementation of national policies for education. At the end of this pioneer research, the Kenya Education Commission envisioned education as a function and instrument for the development of the secular State with the objectives to inculcate among the learners; a sense of nationhood, the values of service to the people without discrimination, respect for the different cultural traditions, respect for human personality, values of social equality and adaptability to change, and the conscious change of attitudes and relationships.[320] Following the recommendations of the Kenya Education Commission, the revised Education Act (1968) transferred the administration of mission schools to Government authorities and relegated the role of missionaries to that of 'sponsor' for the learning institutions they founded.[321] While the sponsor function has metamorphosised over time,[322] it currently entitles the relevant religious denominations to propose representatives to the policy organs[323] and to prepare (for approval) resources for religious instruction in their schools.[324]

Post-independence Kenya also expanded the scope of the religious education to include Christian Religious Education (CRE), Hindu Religious Education (HRE) and Islamic Religious Education (IRE). According to the Kenya Secondary School Curriculum, the general objectives of the CRE syllabus include to enable the learners 'appreciate and respect their own and other people's cultural and Christian beliefs and practices' and 'promote international

---

320 Para 19.

321 Section 8(1) of the Education Act, Chapter 211, Laws of Kenya [Revised Edition 2012 (1980)] for instance provided: 'Where a transferred school was managed by a church, or an organization of churches, and it is the wish of the community served by the school that the religious traditions of the school should be respected, the former manager shall be appointed by the local authority to serve as the sponsor to the school.'

322 For a more general discussion, see Muok, B. Stephen. Joshua. "The "church" as a "sponsor" of education in Kenya: A historical review (1844–2016)." http://www.cihablog.com/church-sponsor-education-kenya-historical-review-1844-2016. Accessed on 21 September 2020.

323 Section 8(1) of the Education Act, Chapter 211, Laws of Kenya [Revised Edition 2012 (1980)] for instance provided: 'Where a transferred school was managed by a church, or an organization of churches, and it is the wish of the community served by the school that the religious traditions of the school should be respected, the former manager shall be appointed by the local authority to serve as the sponsor to the school.' See also Section 29(1)(d) of the Education Act, Chapter 211, Laws of Kenya [Revised Edition 2012 (1980)].

324 Section 8(3) of the Education Act, Chapter 211, Laws of Kenya [Revised Edition 2012 (1980)].

consciousness through the understanding of universal brotherhood and sisterhood'. Relatedly, the IRE syllabus seeks to enable learners 'identify ways in which to foster harmonious co-existence with other people through tolerance' and 'explain ways of promoting international consciousness through an understanding of the universality of Allah and equality of mankind'. In reality however;

> [s]chool leavers exit the system with none of those critical thinking skills that CRE claims to promote, little appreciation of their belief systems within communities, and no ability to make considered moral choices or internalise socially-acceptable behaviour.[325]

Post-independence Nigeria similarly took over all schools through the National Policy on Education[326] and required them to offer both CRK and IRK. In practice, schools in regions predominated by Christians, including those that are publicly supported, continue to offer only CRK and IRC is the only one offered in the regions with Muslim majorities.[327] Only cosmopolitan regions offer both subjects; even then, Christian pupils tend to elect CRK and Muslim pupils prefer IRK hence minimising chances of cross-religious dialogue. That said, it is important to reckon that Nigeria's 1999 Constitution entitles religious denominations that own or run educational institutions to offer religious instruction to students or pupils that are followers of their faith.[328] Obviously, this right privileges mainly the major Christian denominations which have operated educational institutions in the country for nearly two centuries.

Like its African counterparts, post-independence Uganda nationalised all schools (which mainly included Christian missionary schools) through taking charge of the curriculum, funding and the appointment of teaching staff, among other roles.[329] These reforms meant that the educational priorities of Uganda would be 'less evangelical and more national'.[330] They included: 'to address the low levels of literacy; expand primary and school enrolment;

325 Itolondo, Wilfrida. "The role and status of Christian Religious Education in the school curriculum in Kenya." p. 721.

326 Imam, Hauwa. "Educational Policy in Nigeria from the Colonial Era to the Post-Independence Period." *Italian Journal of Sociology of Education*, vol. 1, 2012.

327 Jawaniyi, Oduntan. "Rethinking the Religious Education Curricula in Nigerian Schools." pp. 67–68.

328 Section 38(3), Constitution of Nigeria (1999).

329 See, Nimrod, Muhumuza. *The Constitutionality of Religious Education in Uganda*. pp. 27–28. See, also, Ugandan Education Act, 1963.

330 See, Nimrod, Muhumuza. *The Constitutionality of Religious Education in Uganda*. pp. 4 and 27–28. See, also, Ugandan Education Act, 1963.

improve the standards of technical and agricultural education, and; expand access of opportunities to girls'.[331] As in Kenya, school administration was transferred from the missions to the Government.[332] Nationalisation of schools also entailed that some level of religious instruction equity would be pursued, although only Christian Religious Education and Islamic Religious Education were and are still offered.[333] Most schools founded by religious establishments retained their denominational identities and continue to pursue their original evangelical ends.[334] As recent as 2018, the Education (Pre-Primary, Primary and Post-Primary) Act[335] provides for religious studies as part of the curriculum in primary and post-primary schools but this is understood to only extend to the two Abrahamic religions.

4.3.3 The Wretched African Religion

Throughout the colonial epoch there was no recognition that Africans had their own systems of education prior to the coming of the visitors.[336] Yet religious instruction existed in the African study countries prior to the coming of missionaries. Every African community had its own system of education which also incorporated religious instruction. As Oduntan Jawaniyi rightly stated:

> Contrary to the notion that its population had no education before the earliest contact with the outside world, Nigerians from time immemorial received indigenous forms of education. Traditional/indigenous educational systems in Nigeria, as in other parts of sub-Sahara Africa, prepared individuals to take up their roles as 'cultured' members of their respective society. It offered practical training in indigenous professions. These included native medicine/herbalism, midwifery, priest-crafts, and blacksmithing, among others. Different instructional techniques such as apprenticeships, initiation rites, incantations, dirges, folklores, riddles,

331 See, Nimrod, Muhumuza. *The Constitutionality of Religious Education in Uganda*. pp. 4 and 27–28. See, also, Ugandan Education Act, 1963.

332 See, Nimrod, Muhumuza. *The Constitutionality of Religious Education in Uganda*. pp. 4 and 27–28. See, also, Ugandan Education Act, 1963.

333 See, Nimrod, Muhumuza. *The Constitutionality of Religious Education in Uganda*. pp. 4 and 27–28.

334 See, Nimrod, Muhumuza. *The Constitutionality of Religious Education in Uganda*. pp. 4 and 27–28. See, also, Ugandan Education Act, 1963.

335 The Education (Pre-primary, Primary and Post-Primary) Act, Act No 13 of 2018.

336 See, Nimrod, Muhumuza. *The Constitutionality of Religious Education in Uganda*. p. 26.

> proverbs and experimentations were deployed in the enculturation and vocational training of its people.[337]

According to Wilfrida Itolondo:

> Indigenous African Education was for living. It was concerned with the systematic socialization of the young generation into norms, beliefs, collective opinions of the wider society, practical skills and the acquisition of knowledge which was useful to the individual and the society as a whole.

Indigenous African Education has a lot of religious content and the learning and the faith cannot be separated.[338]

Despite clear evidence of African religious education and its objectives and the post-independence reforms above, the menu of religious instruction in all the African study countries still excludes African religion. In Kenya, notwithstanding the initial resolve not to privilege any particular religion and to respect the religious convictions of all people,[339] matters have not changed in favour of African religion fundamentally. African religious education is not included as an independent subject of Kenya's primary and secondary schools' curriculum although some of its content is integrated with subjects like Christian Religious Education (CRE),[340] History and Literature.[341] It is difficult to reconcile this position with the following finding by the first post-independence Commission of Inquiry into the education sector: –

> Our fifth distinctive contribution had, we felt, to lie in the cultural field. As we listened to our witnesses, we found a very general conviction among them that under colonial government, and more specifically under the influence of the Christian missions, much that was good and important in our indigenous cultures had been lost, or denigrated. This was not only a question of our African arts and crafts, but also of our social institutions

---

337 Jawaniyi, Oduntan. "Rethinking the Religious Education Curricula in Nigerian Schools." pp. 63–64 and 86.

338 Itolondo, Wilfrida. "The Role and Status of Christian Religious Education in the School Curriculum in Kenya," p. 721.

339 The Kenya Education Commission, paragraph, Para 19(c).

340 Beyond two topics, 'African moral and cultural values' and 'Selected aspects in African Religious Heritage' CRE covers little else on African religion.

341 Itolondo, Wilfrida. "The Role and Status of Christian Religious Education in the School Curriculum in Kenya," p. 721.

> and our social relationships. We do not wish for one moment to overlook the artistic side of our culture, but for the purpose of our thinking about education in Kenya it is the customary aspects of our culture that have seemed of the most importance.[342]

As is already clear, the Kenyan situation could be generalised for Nigeria and Uganda quite safely.

There are a number of problems with the approach the African study countries have adopted. To begin with, since it is mainly the Christian missionaries that established modern-style schools and developed formal syllabi for Christian religious education even before the colonial epoch, religious instruction in the African study countries continues to be synonymous with Christian Religious Education. Only Islamic Religious Education is offered in addition to Christian Religious Education and occasionally Hindu Religious Education in the case of Kenya; and instruction in African religion[343] is excluded from the formal educational system meaning that learners can only elect mainly between the two Abrahamic religions.[344] I need not reiterate that the religious instruction offered in missionary schools since the pre-colonial days is not neutral. Its overarching objective was, and remains, to evangelise to the native

342 The Kenya Education Commission, paragraph 10.

343 Ajah Miracles has described indigenous education as follows: "Indigenous education was the earliest type of education, which was offered in the pre-literate era, within the community, by community members who possessed specialized skills or abilities in various fields of human endeavour. Here, boys were mentored by their fathers, or other masters in learning various vocations and etiquette like farming, trading, craftwork, fishing, cattle rearing, wine tapping, traditional medicine and black-smithing, etc. While girls were expected to stay back at home to learn domestic and other chores such as cooking, sweeping, weeding the farmlands, hair weaving, decorations of the body, dye production; and the like from their mothers. This educational tradition is sometimes referred to as precolonial or informal or tribal or community-based education in Africa. There were no schools, professional teachers and absence of students/pupils with uniforms, regimentation and permanent teachers as we have it today in Western education. There were centres for initiation and adult members of society served as teachers. Thus, traditional education, which was nurtured by traditional religions was the process by which every society attempted to preserve and upgrade the accumulated knowledge, skills and attitudes in its cultural setting and heritage to foster continuously the wellbeing of mankind. See, Ajah, Miracle. "Religious Education and Nation-building in Nigeria." *Stellenbosch Theological Journal*, vol. 1, no. 2, 2015, pp. 267–269.

344 See, Nimrod, Muhumuza. *The Constitutionality of Religious Education in Uganda*. p. 3.

Africans.[345] Naturally, this does not augur well for the principles of state-neutrality. As Nimrod Muhumuza rightly notes,

> [S]tate-endorsed religious education that is not taught in an objective and neutral manner that advances the values of tolerance and pluralism runs afoul of the requirement to be neutral towards religion in general and religious education in particular.[346]

Preferential religious education negates the principles of religious equality and inclusivity and the rights of indigenous populations. It also puts non-believers or followers of less dominant religions in an awkward situation whereby they have to study faiths that are alien to them. Preferential programmes also continue the missionary and colonial legacy of perpetuating religious favoritism in educational institutions[347] and disregarding African religion.

The result of the entire set up is a divisive educational system that sometimes acts as a theatre for religious intolerance and violence. Already, religious instruction in Uganda's schools has proven contentious and some learning institutions have experienced faith-inspired violence. In Nigeria, Boko Haram has heightened violent campaigns against westernised education, which it claims lures Muslims away from following their faith and its teachings.[348] On 14/15 April 2014, Boko Haram raided a girl's school in Chibok (part of Borno State) and kidnapped 276 Christian female students allegedly to demonstrate its disdain for western education.[349]

4.4 *The Study Countries and Religious Attire in Educational Institutions*

The study countries apply either restrictive or permissive policies in the regulation of religious attire in educational institutions. France, Turkey (for the most part) and Kenya are restrictive while the US and Nigeria are permissive. The

345 See, Nimrod, Muhumuza. *The Constitutionality of Religious Education in Uganda*. p. 4.

346 Nimrod, Muhumuza. *The Constitutionality of Religious Education in Uganda*. p. 3.

347 See the International Developmental Law Organization. "Freedom of Religion or Belief and the Law: Current Dilemmas and Lessons Learnt." November, 2016, p. 36. See also Gray. Richard. "Christianity, Colonialism, and Communications in Sub-Saharan Africa." *Journal of Black Studies*, vol. 13, no. 1, 1982, pp. 59–72, p. 60.

348 Omede, Jacob and Omede, Andrew Abdul. "Terrorism and insecurity in Nigeria: Moral, values and religious education as panacea." p. 124.

349 "Nigeria Chibok Abductions: What We Know." BBC News, 8 May 2017 https://www.bbc.com/news/world-africa-32299943. Accessed on 21 September 2020.

issue of religious attire in educational institutions has not been sufficiently contested in Uganda to warrant academic analysis.

4.4.1 The Restrictive Approach

After the reforms in Turkey in the last decade, France overtook Turkey as the strictest when it comes to the control of religious attire in schools. Among the African study countries, Kenya leads the way in keeping religious attire out of the schools and Uganda might follow this path.

4.4.1.1 *The Strict France*

The main debate in France has centred on the issue of religious attire in public schools. Between 1989 and 2004, France witnessed a series of controversies relating to the right of Muslim girls to wear *hijab* to public schools. The highest administrative tribunal, *Conseil d'état*, intervened to clarify that students' religious expression was not banned but was instead protected constitutionally.[350] The Conseil d'état directed that the principles of secularism and neutrality "require the State to respect the students' liberty of conscience, meaning that the State should abolish all discrimination by public schools based on their students' religious convictions or beliefs".[351]

However, matters changed in 2004 following the enactment of Law No 2004–228, which provides that 'in public elementary schools, junior high schools and high schools, students are prohibited from wearing signs or clothing through which they exhibit conspicuously a religious affiliation.'[352] This ban covers "'large' Christian crosses, Jewish kippas, and Sikh turbans".[353]

These reforms were informed by the recommendations of a Committee commissioned by President Jacques Chirac, which discouraged public manifestation of religious signs or symbols in educational institutions. The Committee argued that display of religious signs in schools could disturb their ordinary operations. Although the Committee's report applied to all religious symbols, it singled out the hijab because of its association with 'communitarianism'.

350 *Conseil d'état*, No 346.893.

351 Robert, Jacques. "Religious liberty and French secularism." p. 645.

352 Law No 2004–228 of 15 March 2004 concerning, as an application of the principle of the separation of church and state, the wearing of symbols or garb which show religious affiliation in public primary and secondary schools. For a translation and discussion on this law see, Heider. J. "Unveiling the Truth behind the French Burqa Ban: The Unwarranted Restriction of the Right to Freedom of Religion and the European Court of Human Rights." *Indiana International and Comparative Law Review*, vol. 22, 2012, p. 95.

353 Kuru, AT. *Secularism and State Policies toward Religion.* p. 106.

Arguably, communitarianism makes it difficult for teachers to distinguish between "'illicit ostentatious symbols' from 'licit non-ostentatious ones.'" There were also concerns that many Muslim communities force or even abuse girls who do not don the hijab hence the need for their liberation through State policy. As Jeremy Gun notes,

> [t]here is a serious problem of violence against Muslim and Arabic women in France. The most frequently discussed cases have included gang rapes and murders of girls and women in the neighbourhoods in which they live, the perpetrators being men from the same neighbourhoods. In addition, there is strong evidence that many girls and young women are coerced by their families and neighbours into wearing headscarves and other 'non-Western' clothing.[354]

Another reason why hijab has elicited heated debate is because sections of the French population see it as part of the propaganda for a radical and intolerant version of Islam.[355]

The prohibitions put in place by the 2004 law were broadened further by Law No 2010–1192 of 11 October 2010, which prohibits the concealment of the face in public. The 2010 legislation extends the restriction on religious garments to nearly all public spaces 'including streets, markets, private businesses, entertainment venues, Government buildings, and public transportation, but excluding public places of worship.'[356] Any woman caught wearing a face-covering veil is subject to a 150 euro fine or a mandatory French citizenship course. It is also a crime punishable by a 30 000 euro fine and up to a year in prison to force a woman to wear a religious garment.[357] Teachers, much more than their students, are required to adhere to the principle of religious neutrality in which they refrain from offending the conscience of the children under their tutelage.[358] France's policy is clear – to keep religious attires out of public educational institutions.

---

354 Gunn, TJ. "French Secularism as Utopia and Myth." p. 96.

355 Troper, M. "French Secularism, or Laicité." p. 1279.

356 Heider, J. "Unveiling the Truth behind the French Burqa Ban: The Unwarranted Restriction of the Right to Freedom of Religion and the European Court of Human Rights." *Indiana International and Comparative Law Review*, vol. 22, 2012, p. 96.

357 Heider, J. "Unveiling the Truth behind the French Burqa Ban: The Unwarranted Restriction of the Right to Freedom of Religion and the European Court of Human Rights." p. 97.

358 For an exposition of this law, see, Gunn, TJ. "French Secularism as Utopia and Myth.' p. 94.

4.4.1.2 *Turkey Before and the Rise of Islam*

Until October 2013, Turkey enforced a strict official ban on the wearing of hijab in all public and private educational institutions.[359] The rule covered students, faculty and members of staff. Despite being host to a highly religious majority Muslim society,[360] Turkey's resolve to relegate religion to the private outstripped the US, which, as I discuss below, allows students to wear religious symbols, and surpassed France, which bans religious signs only in public schools.[361] This quite combative secular policy was sanctified by the European Court on Human Rights, which, in *Leyla Sahin v Turkey*,[362] agreed with Turkey's policy of restricting the donning of headscarves by female students in institutions of higher learning because it serves greater ends such as the realisation of gender equality, public order and religious toleration.

Even with the approval of the ECHR the question of hijab in universities (and in public service) remained controversial in Turkey. For about three decades it was the subject of intense political contestations. Prime Minister Recep Tayyip Erdogan and his Justice and Development Party rose to power in 2007 waving the promise to lift the ban on hijab. Consequently, on 7 February 2008, Parliament passed a constitutional amendment lifting the ban on hijab in universities by a vote of 79%. But the celebrations were short-lived as the pro-secular Republican People's Party petitioned the Constitutional Court of Turkey claiming that the changes contradicted the secular premises of Turkey's Constitution. About four months later (on 5 June 2008), the Constitutional Court of Turkey annulled the constitutional reforms citing the fact that they offended the founding principles of the secular Constitution.[363] However, the struggles continued and in 2013, Turkey lifted the ban on the headscarf in the

359 Kuru, AT. *Secularism and State Policies toward Religion.* p. 164. The headscarves debate is however, still developing in Turkey. On 8 October 2013, Turkish authorities lifted the ban on headscarves for female workers in state offices. However, the headscarf ban remains in the military, police and judiciary. The matter remains controversial. See, "Turkey lifts long time ban on headscarves in state offices." *New York Times*, 8 October 2013.

360 Judging by church/mosque participation, the Turkish society is more religious than France. Weekly church/mosque participation is only 10 percent in France whereas it is 69 percent in Turkey.

361 Ahmet Kuru observes that historical and contemporary debates on secularism in France, Turkey and the US 'have pointed to education as the main battlefield in state-religion controversies'. See, Kuru, AT. "Passive and Assertive Secularism: Historical Conditions, Ideological Struggles, and State Policies towards Religion." p. 569.

362 *Leyla Sahin v Turkey* (Application No 44774198), judgment of 10 November 2005. Para 105.

363 Roff, Smith. "Why Turkey lifted its ban on the Islamic headscarf" *National Geographic*, 12 October 2013.

universities and public service except for women employed in the military and judicial service.[364] In what appears to be a determinant of this politico-juridical controversy, in December 2018, the Constitutional Court of Turkey ruled for a student who claimed that the headscarf ban had violated her right to education and the right to freedom of religion.[365]

The above changes in Turkey represent the re-emergence of Islam as a major influence on State policy and could be a sign that a significant section of the population no longer holds the strict secular foundations of the Republic.

4.4.1.3 *Kenya's Strict Judicial Policy*

There is a large body of litigation on religious attire and the observance of the days of worship in Kenyan educational institutions. What is common about both is that whenever judges have been asked to weigh between secular school uniform rules and religious teachings, the scales of justice appear to tilt in favour of the former.

In *Republic v the Head Teacher, Kenya High School & Another, ex parte SMY*,[366] a representative application by Muslim students questioned the respondent school's dress code, which did not recognise their religious clothing – the hijab. In its verdict, the High Court recognised the pivotal role played by the right to freedom of thought, conscience and religion in a democratic society but clarified that the entitlement could be qualified under the limitation clause.[367] Lady Justice Cecilia Githua ruled that

> [i]n democratic societies in which several religions co-exist within one another in the same population, it may be necessary to restrict peoples' manifestations of religious beliefs in order to reconcile the interests of the various groups and ensure that every person's beliefs are respected.

Based on these reasons, the High Court preserved the system of school uniform, noting that limitation of the applicant's right to outwardly manifest her religion by wearing a hijab in the educational institution was reasonable and

364 AFP. "Turkey Lifts Decades-old Ban on Headscarves: Measures Allowing Women to Sport the Islamic Head Scarf in State Institutions in part of Broader Package of reforms." https://www.aljazeera.com/news/europe/2013/10/turkey-lifts-decades-old-ban-headscarves-201310814177943704.html. Accessed on 21 September 2020.

365 "Turkey's Constitutional Court rules university headscarf ban violated student's right to education" Daily Sabah, 11 December 2018.

366 [2012] eKLR.

367 The limitation clause is carried under article 24 of the Constitution of Kenya (2010).

justifiable in an open and democratic society based on human dignity, equality and freedom.

The *Kenya High School* case upheld an earlier precedent with similar facts determined under the repealed constitutional order, *Ndanu Mutambuki & 119 Others v Minister for Education and 12 others*,[368] in which High Court judge Joseph Nyamu (as he then was), declined the invitation of a religious sect, *Arata Aroho Mutheru Society*, to compel certain educational institutions to allow members of the religion to attend school in headscarves. Applying Article 78 of the Repealed Constitution, which is largely identical to Article 32 of Kenya's 2010 Constitution, the superior court of record found that the right to freedom of religion is not absolute and must pave the way to public order, morality and health. Justice Nyamu made the following pronouncements on the issue of school dress code:

> In the case of schools, nothing represents the concept of equality more than school uniforms. Unless it is an essential part of faith, it cannot be right for a pupil to get up one morning and decide to put on headscarf as well, this derogates from the hallmarks of a democratic society and violates the principle of equality. In weighing the individual's fundamental right under s 78 against those of others, I find myself unable to disregard the weight of these basic standards and norms and in my view they tilt the scales in favour of a finding of no infringement in the circumstances of this case.

In addition, the High Court emphasised that before an act can be protected as a manifestation of religion it must be proven to constitute a key tenet of the faith in question. Such 'centrality' was not substantiated in the case under review, the Judge held. The ruling also directed that the liberty to determine for a minor a religious denomination is reposted with the parent or guardian rather the spiritual leader of a sect.[369]

---

368 [2007] eKLR.

369 In yet another pre-2010 litigation, *Seventh Day Adventist Church (East Africa) Ltd v Electoral Commission of Kenya*, the High Court resisted the petition to declare a decision by the then electoral management body to hold by-elections on Saturday (a holy day for members of the Seventh Day Adventist Church) a violation of the right to freedom of religion and the right to vote. Justice Githinji (as he then was) grounded his decision on three main pillars: first, that holding elections on Saturday trespassed no known law in Kenya; secondly, that members of the church had a choice either to exercise the right to vote or the freedom of conscience on the date slated for elections; and, finally, that

In *Nyakamba Gekara v Attorney General & 2 others*,[370] the High Court of Kenya ruled against an application that sought to cancel a Parents Teachers Association (PTA) meeting at Kenya High School scheduled on a Saturday. The petitioner submitted that calling for such a crucial meeting on a day of worship for the Adventists, as was the tradition of the school, contravened his right to freedom of worship and was therefore inconsistent with the Constitution. Justice Isaac Lenaola held a different view, that

> [w]hereas the Petitioner has rights under Article 32 of the Constitution, the enjoyment of those rights should not be such that undue hardship in the management of the affairs of the Kenya High School is imposed upon either the 2nd or 3rd Respondents.[371]

Justice Lenaola yet again saved administrators of educational institutions from 'religious-inflicted managerial hardships' in *Seventh Day Adventist Church (East Africa) Limited v Minister for Education & 3 others*.[372] The fundamental question in this case was whether the failure to accommodate the Adventist students' religious manifestations by means of exemption from Saturday classes, examinations and cleaning could be accepted as reasonable and justifiable in an open and democratic society based on human dignity, freedom and equality. The judicial tribunal ruled in the affirmative. It found that

> [i]t is not disputed however that every student has the right to hold whatever religious beliefs his/her conscience dictates. However, manifestations of such beliefs must not injure the rights of the schools they attend to impart education. And if the manifestations of those beliefs is parallel to the rights of the school to impart knowledge on its students, I believe

only the Legislature could determine which days elections can be held. On this basis, the Judge dismissed the application just like the other two discussed above. Miscellaneous Application No 793 of 2001. (2008) 2 KLR (EP).

370 [2013] eKLR. Petition No 82 of 2012. The Petition was between Nyakamba Gekara and the Attorney General, the Chair Parents Teachers Association and the Principal, Kenya High School.

371 Para. 20.

372 [2014] eKLR. Petition No 431 of 2012 between Seventh Day Adventist Church (East Africa) Limited and the Minister for Education (1st Respondent); Attorney General (2nd Respondent); Board of Governors Alliance High School (Interested Party); and National Gender and Equality Commission (Amicus Curiae).

> the right of the students to manifest those beliefs must be limited and that limitation will be justifiable in a free and democratic society …[373]

Justice Lenaola motivated that such limitations 'are not discriminatory as they are applicable to all students from diverse religious beliefs'. Thus, the then High Court judge concluded as follows:

> I have also found that the extent of interference in the enjoyment of the Adventist rights and freedoms is minimized by the reasonable accommodation extended to the SDA students by the Interested Party and I have seen no evidence that other schools have declined to do so. To exempt the Adventist students from the school's programmes would mean to grant them extra accommodation which would in return be cumbersome and chaotic to the Interested Party and other public schools. In my view, the explanation made by Interested Party is sufficient to establish that any infringement of the rights to religion is reasonable and justifiable in accordance with Article 24 of the Constitution.[374]

It took the Court of Appeal in *Mohamed Fugicha v Methodist Church in Kenya (suing through its registered trustees) & 3 others*[375] to attempt a different narrative. In this decision, justices Philip Waki, Roselyn Nambuye and Patrick Kiage established that allowing Muslim girls to wear hijab did not discriminate against non-Muslim students and ordered the recognition of religious attire in the design of school uniforms as part of Kenya's education policy. The Court of Appeal reasoned that to force students to abandon a practice dear to them and genuinely held as a manifestation of their religious convictions violates their conscience. When it stood, the judgement overruled a High Court decision which had found in favour of standard school uniform policy.[376] The High Court had issued an injunction preventing St Pauls Kiwanjani Day Mixed Secondary School (the respondents) from implementing a policy allowing Muslim girl students to wear hijab, white trousers and open shoes holding that discriminatory, unlawful, unconstitutional and contrary to the school rules and regulations.

373 Para. 73.
374 Para. 75.
375 [2016] eKLR.
376 *Methodist Church (Suing through its registered trustees) v Teachers Service Commission & 2 others* [2015] eKLR, Petition No 030 of 2014.

The Court of Appeal's quite revolutionary judgement overlooked a procedural technicality concerning the filing of cross-petitions,[377] which the Supreme Court would later use as the basis for disallowing the entire thread of litigations. Thus in *Methodist Church in Kenya v Mohamed Fugicha & 3 others*,[378] despite recognising the importance of the issue contained in the impugned cross-petition, the Supreme Court maintained that:

> [I]t is imperative that the matter ought to reach us in the proper manner, so that when a party seeks redress from this court, they ought to have had the matter properly instituted, the issues canvassed and determined in the professionally competent chain of courts leading up to this Apex Court. In view of this, it is our recommendation that should any party wish to pursue this issue, they ought to consider instituting the matter formally at the High Court.[379]

However, Justice Jackton Ojwang's dissenting opinion ignored the procedural technicalities and upheld the findings of the Court of Appeal 'that the concepts of justice, fairness or reasonableness would not only permit, but in fact do require, differential treatment'.[380] Justice Ojwang described this position as 'appositely pragmatic and rational, and well reflects the desirable judicial stand,'[381] holding further that:

> It is in that context that I now interpret the terms of Section 27 (d) of the Basic Education Act, 2013 (Act No. 14 of 2013): imposing upon a school's sponsor (such as the petitioner herein) the obligation of "maintenance of spiritual development while safeguarding the denominations or religious adherence of others". [95] It is my standpoint, in departure from the Bench majority, that all the applicable terms of the Constitution and of the enacted law, do entail the finding – precisely in keeping with that of the Appellate Court – that a right balance amidst people holding

377 The majority judgement of the Supreme Court stated: "Furthermore and with due respect to the Appellate Court, we are persuaded that the cross-petition was improperly before the High Court, and ought not to have been introduced by an interested party, and in that light, it should not and could not have been entertained by the Court of Appeal; neither court having proper jurisdiction to do so." Paragraph 58.

378 [2019] eKLR.

379 Para. 59.

380 Para. 91.

381 Para. 91.

> different faiths, in the multi-cultural environment prevailing at the pertinent school, will by no means be jeopardized on account of the variation to the school dress-code. I would, therefore, have dismissed the appeal.[382]

Had Justice Ojwang's edict stood, it would have directed St Paul's Kiwanjani Day Mixed Secondary School to amend the rules relating to dress-code to accommodate those students whose religious beliefs require them to wear, in addition to regular uniform, certain particular items of clothing.[383] It would also have required

> [t]he Cabinet Secretary in charge of the education to sustain the formulation and application of appropriate rules, regulations or directions – so designed as to uphold the fundamental rights of the Constitution on matters of belief and of religion, of equality, and of freedom from discrimination, as prescribed in Article 27 and 32, and in respect of all schooling establishments in relevant counties.[384]

I have discussed these cases to demonstrate the influence of British colonialism and French and Turkish secularism on Kenya's judicial jurisprudence. My argument is that while international human rights law guarantees the freedom to manifest one's religion, judicial jurisprudence in Kenya is in favour of religion-free school rules and dress codes as in France and in Turkey during the material time. No wonder nearly all of the cases I discuss above cite *Leyla Sahin v Turkey* with approval.[385] For instance, the *Ndanu Mutambuki* case advocated that *Leyla Sahin v Turkey* should serve as a persuasive authority because Article 9 of the European Convention on Human Rights was similar to Section 78 of Kenya's Repealed Constitution. Kenyan courts also consider *Kalac v Turkey*[386] and *Karaduman v Turkey*[387] persuasive authorities. Kenya's Court of Appeal complained about such interpretations because they

---

382 Paras. 94–95.

383 Para. 96.

384 Para. 97.

385 See, for instance, *Ndanu Mutambuki & 119 Others v Minister for Education and 12 others, Seventh Day Adventist Church (East Africa) Limited v Minister for Education & 3 others, and Republic v the Head Teacher, Kenya High School & Another, ex parte SMY Methodist Church in Kenya v Mohamed Fugicha & 3 others.*

386 Application No 20704/92 in the European Court of Human Rights.

387 (1993) 74 DR 93.

> [s]eem to take too far the notion of secularism in a manner suggestive of hostility to religion that is discordant with the letter and spirit of the Constitution and the most progressive jurisprudence on the subject.[388]

The requirements of African religion and Islam on the dress code are clearly incompatible with the policies of the learning institutions, most of which continue to operate under the fairly Christianised missionary and colonial policies. Both in the rule against religious attire and in the policy for religious instruction, African religion (and Africanised religious groups like Arata Aroho Mutheru) and Islam yield to Christianity and the secular culture socialised around it. Fringe Christian denominations, like the Adventists, may also have accumulated sufficient grievances against the State.

As in Kenya, the secular goals that underpin public educational institutions reign over competing religious beliefs to which the learners might subscribe in Uganda – at least from the judicial point of view. In this regard, the justices of the Supreme Court of Uganda[389] preserved a Makerere University policy requiring students to attend classes, take mandatory tests and examinations on any day of the week, including Saturday, holding that the right to freedom of religion ought to be enjoyed alongside the secular goals for which educational institutions are established. The Supreme Court of Uganda made this finding notwithstanding evidence to the effect that for the Adventists observance of the Sabbath is one of the Ten Commandments.[390] The judges were satisfied that as long as the students were notified of the university policy and regulations beforehand, there was no violation of their right for they had an early opportunity to transfer to another institution whose policies matched

388 *Mohamed Fugicha v Methodist Church in Kenya (suing through its registered trustees) & 3 others* [2016] eKLR.

389 In a constitutional petition between Dimanche Sharon, Mokera Gilphine and Nansereko Luck and Makerere University before the Supreme Court of Uganda, dated 1 August 2006. Constitutional Appeal No 2 of 2004. In the Supreme Court of Uganda at Mengo; before Odoki, CJ, Oder, Tsekooko, Karokora, Mulenga, Kanyeihamba and Katureebe, JJ.SC. The case was an appeal from the decision of the Constitutional Court dated 24 September 2003, in Constitutional Petition No 1 of 2003.

390 The Book of Exodus spells out as follows: "Remember the Sabbath Day by keeping it holy. Six days you shall labour and do all your work but the Seventh Day is a Sabbath to the Lord your God. On it you shall not do any work, neither you, nor your son or daughter nor your man-servant nor your maid-servant nor your animals nor the alien within your gates. For in six days the Lord made the heavens and the earth, the sea, and all that is in them, but he rested on the seventh day. Therefore, the Lord blessed the Sabbath Day and made it holy." See, Chapter 20, verses 8–11.

their religious doctrine. Belying this finding is the reality that religious equity is not one of the underlying values of Uganda's education system. For example, Uganda's school calendar recognises only four religious holidays that correspond to the dominant denominations: Christmas, Easter, Ramadhan, and Martyr's Day.[391] Thus, in the absence of litigation on religious attire in Uganda, this background helps us anticipate that courts are likely to adopt a restrictive approach when the question emerges finally.

4.4.2 The Permissive Approach

Although US policies are tough on religious instruction, they are tender on the dress code for the US does not prohibit the wearing of headscarves or any other religious garments in public schools.[392]

Similarly, Nigeria's judicial jurisprudence supports a permissive school dress code. Citing Article 45(1) of the Constitution, which is about limitations of human rights, the High Court of Nigeria (in *The Provost, Kwara State College of Education, Ilorin & ORS v Basirat Saliv & ORS*) upheld limitations on the donning of hijab by female college students. But the Court of Appeal of Nigeria disagreed with the lower court, arguing that such kerbs violate the free exercise of religion. Again, in *Asiyat Abdulkareem & ORS v Lagos State Government & ORS*,[393] the Court of Appeal overturned a High Court decision that had held that the wearing of hijab in a secular school infringes on the right of non-Muslim students because they end up feeling inferior to the hijab-wearing students. Although religious dress in educational institutions is legal in Nigeria; like in Turkey and Kenya, the issue is highly contested and remains an area where constant and even abrupt changes can be expected.

By legalising the headscarf in educational institutions, Nigeria has created the stage for the full-flowering of the triple heritage since practitioners of traditional African religion and Islam may manifest their religious convictions freely. However, like in Kenya, its religious instruction policy favours only the two dominant Abrahamic religions with the exception that Islam may have a stronger bargain particularly in Northern Nigeria.

---

391 Reuben, Musiime. "A Critical Evaluation of The Religious Education Curriculum for Secondary School Students In Uganda", dissertation presented to the Graduate Council of the University of North Texas in partial fulfillment of the requirements for the degree of Doctor of Philosophy, December 1996. Page 16.

392 Allen, Anita. L. "Undressing Difference: The Hijab in the West." *The Politics of the Veil* (*The Public Square*). Edited by Scott. Wallah. Joan, Princeton University Press, 2007, p. 210.

393 *Asiyat Abdulkareem & ORS v Lagos State Government & ORS* (2016) 15 NWLR.

Part 5: Conclusion and Way Forward

The central hypothesis of this contribution is that the African study countries apply the principle of state-secularism based, firstly, on the colonial legacy and, secondly, on a warped appreciation of the experiences of their northern counterparts without considering the dynamics of their own triple heritage which in this case includes African religion, Islam and Christianity. The result is a disturbing alienation of African religion and Islam causing both ethno-religious conflicts and struggles for religious equality.

After explaining the conceptual framework for this study, I surveyed secular state practice in the study countries based on three main indicators – the subjugation of religion to secular principles, the degree of inclusiveness of state identity, and the basis for formulating state policies. This discussion found that the cumulative practices of the study countries varies greatly to the extent of obfuscating any consistent patterns. For example, while I found France and Turkey to have national emblems that are nearly free from religion, the countries support religious activities through public funding. The US has religious national emblems, but it does not fund religious activities – in principle. I also found that the various policies of the northern study countries respond to their particular historical circumstances and this has sometimes meant accommodating religion in the public sphere. The lesson for the African study countries is that they need not be bound by any particular policies in the state-secularism paradigm; and they should be free to adopt the most appropriate policies for their historical circumstances – in this regard the triple heritage. The African study countries must also not aim to eliminate religion from the public sphere since this is not only undesirable but also an impossibility.

I then tested the central hypothesis using the right to freedom of religion in educational institutions. My finding is that despite ratifying the major international human rights instruments, and constitutionalising their provisions on the right to freedom of religion, including the freedom to manifest religious belief, emerging judicial jurisprudence in Kenya and Uganda militates against open manifestation of religion, say, through religious attire (in Kenya) and through observance of the Sabbath (in Kenya and Uganda). All the African study countries permit religious instruction but this only applies to christianity, islam and – in a limited sense – Hindu (in the case of Kenya). Moreover, all the African study countries continue the colonial legacy of using the mostly westernised or arabised educational platforms as forums for evangelism.[394]

394 Albeit with some modifications.

Consistent with the earlier finding, state practice on both aspects under review – religious attire and religious instruction – is neither uniform nor consistent. In this regard, it is possible to draw parallels between the northern comparators and the African study countries in relation to how they regulate religion in educational institutions. While Turkey upholds an accommodative policy towards religious instruction in public schools and strict secular rules against religious dress codes (for the most part), the US maintains a zero-tolerance policy against religious instruction and a liberal dress code in educational institutions. France is tough on both religious instruction and dress code, which makes it the stricter country when it comes to suppressing public manifestation of religion. In the African study countries (like in Turkey), controlled religious instruction in educational institutions is permissible since the colonial epoch, but religious rules and dress codes are struggling to find a comfortable place particularly in Kenya and Uganda. Although Nigeria is an exception, its Court of Appeal has set aside lower court decisions that ruled against the hijab in schools, a sign that the restrictive approach to religious dressing is held there as well. Despite having the latitude to adopt either the accommodative or restrictive approaches on both issues without offending the tradition of state-secularism, the African study countries incline towards policies that subordinate African religion.

Due to historical reasons, the mainstream Christian denominations are the beneficiaries of educational policies in the African study countries while the practitioners of African religion (and sometimes Islam, Hindu, fringe Christian faiths like the Seventh Day Adventists and other minor religious groups) are the main losers. The Christian faith benefits mainly because its missionaries seized the colonial epoch to consolidate their ownership and control of educational institutions. This advantage continued in the post-independence era with the maintenance of both the Christian content in the curriculum and the missionary stewardship of educational institutions. It is useful to reiterate at this point that the age of the enlightenment and related revolutions cultured the Christian religion to co-exist with today's secular states. When understood as deferring to Caesar in temporal matters, the concept of state-secularism itself is easily a Christian principle. Additionally, during the era of Christendom, Christian principles penetrated the legal systems of Europe, which in turn introduced the value-laden legal systems to the African study countries during the colonial epoch as part of the secular legal order. These Christian values remain embedded in the legal systems of the African study countries to date.

Condemnation of public manifestation of religion negatively affects the practitioners of African religion because their faith accompanies them in every aspect including in educational institutions, and they are sometimes required to express their beliefs by donning in a manner that may fail the western or secular test of formality. African religion also loses because it is not part of the main curriculum in all the African study countries. Hence my deduction that both where religious manifestation in educational institutions is denied, as in the case of religious attire in Kenya, and where it is accepted, as in the case of religious instruction in all the African study countries, African religion suffers cultural alienation.

I also found that the restrictive dress code in Kenya's educational institutions is based on a common but mistaken understanding of the concept of state-secularism, which equates it to animosity toward external manifestation of religion. In this regard, the reforms in France since 2004 (consolidating policies aimed at eliminating religious manifestation from the public sphere) and Turkey (until October 2013) could have influenced Kenya's initial judicial jurisprudence on religious attire. The changes in Turkey in the last decade (providing for a more liberal dress code) could have influenced recent attempts to review judicial policy in Kenya.

Given the context above, state-religion policies of the African study countries require to reflect their historical and current realities in which the triple heritage plays a prominent role. In this regard, I propose that the best way to realise the full flowering of the triple heritage is to erect the three pillars of Charles Taylor's definition of state-secularism, which in this case should entail i) the freedom to have and to manifest religious beliefs, ii) equal treatment of religion, and iii) and efforts toward an all-inclusive state identity.

The first pillar should entitle everyone to belong to a religion (or not to belong) and to practice its teachings subject only to the acceptable limitations meant to protect public safety, order, health or morals or the fundamental rights and freedoms of others. Religious freedom should also protect faithfuls from unnecessary limitations on the right to express themselves through donning particular religious attire or observing sacred days among others. The application of religious freedom in the African study countries should also appreciate the unique character of African religion, especially its vibrancy, its public requirements and that it covers the entire life cycle of its adherents.

The second pillar should not only accord equality to every religious group but also deny unreasonable advantage to any of them. That said, I suggest that the dispensation of religious equality in Africa should be alive to the devastating effects of the colonial epoch on indigenous cultures and religion and should therefore train its focus on certain affirmative measures to restore the wretched faith. In this respect, affirmative action measures may entail state involvement in measures such as the development of African Religious Education curriculum or the promotion of indigenous values.

The third pillar calls for a rainbow nation of sorts where all religious formations are not only included as part of the national identity but also feel so. Although the triple heritage is a good place to begin that conversation, the framework should be expanded to include Baha'i, Judaism, Hinduism, atheists, and agnostics, among other beliefs, all that have become African religions.

www.ingramcontent.com/pod-product-compliance
Lightning Source LLC
Chambersburg PA
CBHW031332230926
51848CB00001B/208
9789004446410